The University of Georgia

First-year Composition Guide

2011 Edition

D1318887

FOUNTAINHEAD
PRESS

Our Green initiatives include:

Electronic Products
We deliver products in non-paper form whenever possible. This includes pdf download-ables, flash drives, & CDs.

Electronic Samples
We use Xample, a new electronic sampling system. Instructor samples are sent via a personalized web page that links to pdf downloads.

FSC Certified Printers
All of our printers are certified by the Forest Service Council which promotes environ-mentally and socially responsible management of the world's forests. This program allows consumer groups, individual consumers, and businesses to work together hand-in-hand to promote responsible use of the world's forests as a renewable and sustainable resource.

Recycled Paper
Most of our products are printed on a minimum of 30% post-consumer waste recycled paper.

Support of Green Causes
When we do print, we donate a portion of our revenue to green causes. Listed below are a few of the organizations that have received donations from Fountainhead Press. We welcome your feed-back and suggestions for contributions, as we are always searching for worthy initiatives.

Rainforest 2 Reef
Environmental Working Group

Book design by Susan Moore
Cover Design by Doris Bruey
Cover Photo by Rick O'Quinn

Books may be purchased for educational purposes.

For information, please call or write:

1-800-586-0330
Fountainhead Press
Southlake, TX. 76092

Web site: www.fountainheadpress.com
Email: customerservice@fountainheadpress.com

Fourth Edition

ISBN: 978-1-59871-515-6

Printed in the United States of America

Table of Contents

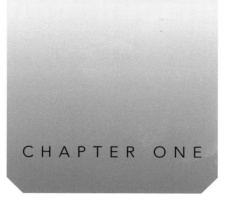

CHAPTER ONE

Introduction to First-year Composition

First-year Composition Program

Office: 128 Park Hall
Telephone: (706) 542-2128

Administration
Dr. Christy Desmet, Director
Dr. Deborah Church Miller, Associate Director
Dr. Allison Lenhardt, Assistant Director
Ms. Beth Beggs, Assistant Director, UGA Writing Center
Ms. Jane Barroso, Administrative Assistant II (jbarroso@uga.edu)

Why Write? FYC and Academic Discourse

Writing is more than simply recording our thoughts, observations, and conclusions. Often it is a way of discovering what we think or feel. If it were merely the transcribing of what is in our minds, writing would never cause us any problems. Yet how many times have you sat down to write, thinking you knew what you wanted to express, only to find that your thoughts were jumbled or half-formed? Or you may have begun a writing assignment with nothing to say, but found, as you wrote, that you had a range of opinions and information about your subject. In both cases, you discovered what you actually knew or thought only in the act of writing.

Scholars and researchers have long known that writing is itself "a way of knowing." The act of writing improves comprehension of academic material and fixes that material in our memories. This benefit of using writing to master and recall information is discussed further in Robert Leamnson's brief essay, "Learning (Your First Job)," which is included in this book. Even more important, writing can play an important role in the *process* of learning itself. Writing helps us to make connections among different pieces of information and between information and ideas; it also provides us with a visible record of those connections and (for instance, in the case of multiple drafts) shows us how our ideas change over time. In Leamnson's terms, writing allows us to produce not just "information," but "knowledge."

The kind of writing focused on in First-year Composition (FYC) is called academic discourse. At the University of Georgia, you will be asked to do many different kinds of writing for your classes. As you move into your academic major toward graduation, you will become increasingly involved in writing tasks that draw on specific genres and conventions for your academic field. Psychologists, for instance, engage in different kinds of research and writing than do literary critics. First-year Composition cannot prepare you directly for all these advanced experiences in writing; what we do instead is to give you a grounding in academic discourse, which lays a foundation for later thinking and writing experiences by practicing kinds of writing that seek to inform and persuade a range of audiences. In FYC courses, you will do research on various topics and, together with your teacher and fellow students, work through writing and discussion to use that information to produce knowledge. You will also test the persuasiveness of your knowledge for a variety of audiences, including your teacher, peers, and others.

Two other important goals of FYC are the arts of revision and collaborative critique. For each writing assignment, FYC classes engage in drafting and revision, and for each they engage as well in peer review. You get the opportunity to demonstrate your proficiency in these two crucial areas in the Composing/Revision and Peer Review exhibits in the Electronic Portfolio that you submit as your final requirement in the course. (The Electronic Portfolio is discussed in detail later in this book.) Your skill in these areas will stand you in good stead as you leave your current teacher and classmates, moving through the core curriculum and your chosen major at the University of Georgia. Finally, our program emphasizes writing in the new electronic environments that are important not only to academics and the world of business, but also to individuals in their private lives. You will experience a variety of technologies in FYC, including the program's own electronic writing environment, <emma>™, which we use both for work during the semester and for constructing final FYC Electronic Portfolios.

The Instructors and Administration of UGA's First-year Composition Program sincerely hope that you enjoy your experiences with writing this year and that you leave our program with the skills and work habits necessary to succeed in writing tasks throughout the curriculum and in the world of work. More broadly, we hope that you leave us feeling confident of your critical thinking, your composing and revision skills, and your ability to comment intelligently on your own and others' writing. Finally, we hope that you will continue to enjoy and practice writing during your years at the University of Georgia. For that reason, we will give you information later about further opportunities for reading and writing at UGA.

CHAPTER TWO

Description of First-year Composition Courses

2

All FYC courses share a set of core goals, or learning outcomes, which are detailed below and are also reflected in the Program Grading Rubric and capstone Electronic Portfolio assignment (both of which are discussed in greater detail later in this *Guide*).

English 1101:
First-year Composition I

English 1101 focuses on informational, analytical, and argumentative writing (the principal genres of academic discourse that students will encounter in many courses across the curriculum), and on research skills and critical thinking. While there are different varieties of English 1101 classes and instructors design their own syllabi, you can get a general sense of what an English 1101 course looks like by consulting the ENGL 1101 Sample Syllabi posted on the First-year Composition Program's website, available online through the English Department Home Page at: http://www.english.uga.edu/.

Prerequisites:
Students must either place into English 1101 or pass out of the Academic Enhancement Program.

Goals:
In English 1101 students will learn to:
- write papers in and out of class using processes that include discovering ideas and evidence, organizing that material, and revising, editing, and polishing the finished paper;
- think critically so that they can recognize the difference between opinion and evidence and so that they can support a complex, challenging thesis;
- address papers to a range of audiences;
- understand the collaborative and social aspects of the writing process and demonstrate an ability to critique the writing of themselves and others;

- develop a sense of voice appropriate to the subject, the writer's purpose, the context, and the reader's expectations;
- understand how genres shape reading and writing and produce writing in several genres;
- follow the conventions of standard edited English and MLA documentation;
- use electronic environments for drafting, reviewing, revising, editing, and sharing texts;
- understand and exploit the differences in the rhetorical strategies and in the affordances available for both print and electronic composing processes and texts.

Requirements:
Students will write a minimum of three essays (1,000-1,500 words or longer) that count for at least 50% of the student's final grade. In addition to writing papers and doing other work, all students will create a final electronic portfolio that counts approximately as one-third of their final grade. The ePortfolio is discussed at greater length below.

Course Texts:
Lunsford, ed. *The St. Martin's Handbook*, 7th ed.
Rosenwasser and Stephen, *Writing Analytically*, 6th ed.
First-year Composition Guide, 2011 ed. (Fountainhead Press)
Any standard college dictionary, such as:
American Heritage Dictionary
Random House College Dictionary
Webster's New Collegiate Dictionary
Webster's New World Dictionary

English 1102:
First-year Composition II

Prerequisites:
To enroll in English 1102, students must have either exempted English 1101 or passed it with a "D" or better. To graduate, however, students must have earned a grade of "C" in English 1101 and have a combined average grade of "C" in English 1101 and 1102/1102M. Students therefore are strongly advised not to enroll in English 1102/1102M until they have received a "C" in English 1101.

According to the University policy on plus-minus grading, a grade of "C-" will not satisfy the requirement for a "C" in ENGL 1101; a combined average of "C-" or 1.7 in English 1101 and 1102 will not satisfy the requirement for a combined average of "C" in the two courses. For more information on plus-minus grading, see: http://www. bulletin.uga.edu/PlusMinusGradingFAQ.html. FAQ #9 is particularly relevant to the requirements of First-year Composition.

Goals:

English 1102 shares the core goals, or learning outcomes, of English 1101, but includes as well other goals specific to the course. The content also varies: while English 1101 focuses on different varieties of non-fiction writing, English 1102 focuses on informational, analytical, and argumentative writing through literary texts in various genres; as in English 1101 and English 1102M, research and critical thinking skills are also emphasized. While there are different varieties of English 1102 classes and instructors design their own syllabi, you can get a general sense of what an English 1102 course looks like by consulting the ENGL 1102 Sample Syllabi posted on the First-year Composition Program's website, available online through the English Department Home Page at: http://www.english.uga.edu/.

In English 1102 students will learn to:
- read fiction, drama, and poetry and write analytically about them;
- understand literary principles and use basic terms important to critical writing and reading;
- write papers in and out of class using processes that include discovering ideas and evidence, organizing that material, and revising, editing, and polishing the finished paper;
- think critically so that they can recognize the difference between opinion and evidence and so that they can support a complex, challenging thesis, and more specifically, document essays using textual evidence;
- address papers to a range of audiences;
- understand the collaborative and social aspects of the writing process and demonstrate an ability to critique the writing of themselves and others;
- develop a sense of voice appropriate to the subject, the writer's purpose, the context, and the reader's expectations;
- understand how genres shape reading and writing and produce writing in several genres;
- follow the conventions of standard edited English and MLA documentation;
- use electronic environments for drafting, reviewing, revising, editing, and sharing texts;
- understand and exploit the differences in the rhetorical strategies and in the affordances available for both print and electronic composing processes and texts.

Requirements:

Students will write a minimum of three essays (1,000-1,500 words or longer) that count for at least 50% of the student's final grade. In addition to writing papers and doing other work, all students will create a final electronic portfolio that counts approximately as one-third of their final grade. The ePortfolio is discussed at greater length below.

Course Texts:

Lunsford, ed. *The St. Martin's Handbook*, 7th ed.

Clifford and Schilb, eds. *Making Literature Matter*, 4th ed., or Desmet, Hart, and Miller, eds., *Prentice Hall Literature Portfolio*, or another approved text of the instructor's choice

First-year Composition Guide, 2011 ed. (Fountainhead Press)

Any standard college dictionary, such as:

American Heritage Dictionary

Random House College Dictionary

Webster's New Collegiate Dictionary

Webster's New World Dictionary

English 1102M:
Multicultural First-year Composition II

Description:

English 1102M focuses on developing effective critical writing, reading, and research skills using core texts that explore the multicultural dimensions of American literature and culture, with an emphasis on African American, Latino/a American, Asian-American, and/or Native American literary traditions. This course offers three hours of credit toward the First-year Composition requirement and satisfies the Franklin College Multicultural Literacy requirement. While English 1102M instructors design their own syllabi, you can get a general sense of what an English 1102M course looks like by consulting the ENGL 1102M Sample Syllabi posted on the First-year Composition Program's website, available online through the English Department Home Page at: http://www.english.uga.edu/.

Goals:

In English 1102M students will learn to:

- read fiction, drama, and poetry—with an emphasis on African American, Latino/a American, Asian-American, and/or Native American literary traditions—and write analytically about them;

- situate literature in the historical and cultural context of production and reception;
- understand literary principles and use basic terms important to critical writing and reading;
- write papers in and out of class using processes that include discovering ideas and evidence, organizing that material, and revising, editing, and polishing the finished paper;
- think critically so that they can recognize the difference between opinion and evidence and so that they can support a complex, challenging thesis, and more specifically, document essays using textual evidence;
- address papers to a range of audiences;
- understand the collaborative and social aspects of the writing process and demonstrate an ability to critique the writing of themselves and others;
- develop a sense of voice appropriate to the subject, the writer's purpose, the context, and the reader's expectations;
- understand how genres shape reading and writing and produce writing in several genres;
- follow the conventions of standard edited English and MLA documentation;
- use electronic environments for drafting, reviewing, revising, editing, and sharing texts;
- understand and exploit the differences in the rhetorical strategies and in the affordances available for both print and electronic composing processes and texts.

Requirements:

Students will write a minimum of three essays (1,000-1,500 words or longer) that count for at least 50% of their final grade. In addition to writing papers and doing other work, all students will create a final electronic portfolio that counts approximately as one-third of their final grade. The ePortfolio is discussed at greater length below.

Course Texts:

Lunsford, ed. *The St. Martin's Handbook*, 7th ed.

Schmidt and Crockett, eds., *Portable Legacies* or another approved text of the instructor's choice

First-year Composition Guide, 2011 ed. (Fountainhead Press)

Any standard college dictionary, such as:

American Heritage Dictionary

Random House College Dictionary

Webster's New Collegiate Dictionary

Webster's New World Dictionary

Honors Courses for First-year Composition II

Description:

Honors students have the option of substituting for English 1102 either English 1050H (Composition and Literature) or English 1060H (Composition and Multicultural Literature). These courses have the same general goals as other First-year Composition courses at the University of Georgia, but each class is designed individually by the instructor, often around a special topic.

English Composition for ESOL Students

Description:

Special sections of English 1101 and 1102/1102M are reserved for students who have a native language other than American English and who can benefit from an English for Speakers of Other Languages (ESOL) emphasis in these classes. Students enroll only with the permission of the department (POD), but the classes are not marked differently on their transcripts. The ESOL sections, like classes for native speakers, focus on writing academic argument in English 1101 and writing about literature in English 1102/1102M. In addition to offering three hours of credit toward the First-year Composition requirement, English 1102M ESOL will also fulfill the Franklin College Multicultural Literacy requirement.

First-year Composition classes for ESOL offer non-native speakers opportunities for vocabulary development, for grammar practice, and for orientation to American styles of writing and organization. Residents of the United States whose first language is not American English, as well as international students, may qualify for these classes. To determine your eligibility and to obtain a POD to register for the ESOL classes, contact the First-year Composition Program Office (706-542-2128) or Jane Barroso at jbarroso@uga.edu.

First-year Composition Online

Description:

Often, the FYC Program offers several English 1101 and 1102/1102M sections taught via the Internet and the World Wide Web. First-year Composition Online has the same goals and requirements as other FYC classes at the University of Georgia: our version of the course has an additional advantage in that it asks students to communicate through writing frequently and in different contexts. FYC courses at the University of Georgia are synchronous – that is, students meet virtually in class at designated class times each week.

Alternative Approaches to First-year Composition

The First-year Composition Program is involved in a number of innovative programs on campus and offers several alternative versions of its core courses. Each of these courses has the same prerequisites, goals, and requirements as the more traditional versions.

- **Special Topics:** Experienced instructors may design a special topics version of FYC that is approved in advance by the First-year Composition Committee. These courses often focus on topics related to the instructor's research or scholarly interests, and the sections are marked by a special note in OASIS.

- **UGA Learning Communities**: The FYC Program has played a major role in the development of UGA's Learning Communities. As part of each Learning Community, students take a First-year Composition class that is linked to the theme of the LC and sometimes to the content of their other courses in the LC. A description of the UGA Learning Communities and a current list of LC's being offered may be found online at: http://www.uga.edu/learningcommunities/.

- **FYC in the Franklin Residential College:** Each Fall semester the FYC Program offers one section of First-year Composition for the Franklin Residential Community. This special class is designed specifically for the community by the instructor. For more information on the FRC, see http://www.uga.edu/frc/.

- **Reacting to the Past:** The FYC Program frequently offers sections of composition that incorporate the innovative pedagogy of UGA's Reacting to the Past curriculum. You can find out more about Reacting at the University of Georgia at: http://www.reacting.uga.edu/.

Policies and Procedures

3

Placement

Most university students will take English 1101 and 1102/1102M during their first year at UGA. However, some students will receive credit for these courses based on the following tests. Complete information about Placement is available on the Registrar's website, under the heading "Credit from Testing," at: http://www.reg.uga.edu/creditFromTesting.

1. **The Advanced Placement Test**: Students who earn a score of 3 or 4 on the National Advanced Placement Test in Literature and Composition or Language and Composition receive three hours of credit for English 1101; those who earn a score of 5 receive six hours of credit for English 1101 and 1102. All AP equivalencies are available on the Registrar's website: http://www.reg.uga.edu/creditFromTesting/advancedPlacement/uga_ap_credit_equivalencies.

2. **The International Baccalaureate (IB) Test**: Students who earn a score of 4, 5, or 6 on the International Baccalaureate Test at the Higher Level (HL) in English receive three hours of credit for English 1101; those who earn a score of 7 on the International Baccalaureate Test at the Higher Level (HL) receive six hours of credit for English 1101 and 1102. Students who earn a score of 5, 6, or 7 on the Standard Level (SL) test receive three hours of credit for English 1101. All IB equivalencies are available on the Registrar's website: http://www.reg.uga.edu/creditFromTesting/internationalBaccalaureate/uga_ib_credit_equivalencies.

3. **The Departmental Placement Test**: Beginning in Fall 2003, students not placed by a national placement test will fall into two groups. Students with an SATV score of 590 and above or an ACT score of 26 or above will place automatically in ENGL 1101 and may register for that class without any further testing; if these students choose to do so, they may take the Departmental Placement Test voluntarily with an eye to exempting English 1101 with three hours of credit. Students with an SATV score of 580 or below who have not been placed by a national placement test are **required** to take the Departmental Placement Test before registering for a First-year Composition class.

Specific information about the Departmental English Placement Test can be found at the Testing Services Website: http://testing.uga.edu/english.php.

The Departmental English Placement Test consists of two parts, mechanics and rhetoric. A score of 22 (part 1) and 20 (part 2) will place students in English 1102 and give them three hours of credit for English 1101. Students whose test scores indicate that they might have trouble in English 1101 will write an essay to determine whether they will be advised to take English 1101 or an Academic Enhancement class.

Students should take the test at a First-year Orientation Session. Those who miss the test at Orientation may take it later at University Testing Services in Clark Howell Hall. However, the test is not open to students who have taken or are currently enrolled in First-year Composition here or elsewhere. For more information, please call (706) 542-3183 or visit the website: http://testing.uga.edu.

Absences

Because writing skills develop slowly over time and because in-class activities are crucial to the final Portfolio, students' regular attendance is essential in First-year Composition. Consequently, on the **fifth** absence (MWF classes) or the **fourth** absence (TTh classes), no matter what the reason, students can expect to be dropped either with a WP or a WF before the midpoint of the semester and with a WF after midpoint. For summer session, on the **fourth** absence, no matter what the reason, students can expect to be dropped either with a WP or a WF before the midpoint of the semester and with a WF after midpoint.

Grade Appeals

It is the instructor's responsibility to judge work and assign grades. Consequently, students with questions about final grades should first discuss those questions with their instructors. If the problem cannot be resolved in discussion, students may prepare a grade appeal in writing according to the new guidelines established by the Franklin College Bylaws, Article V. The bylaws are available at: http://www.franklin.uga.edu/fac_staff/govern/bylaws.htm. Search for "Grade Appeals."

In First-year Composition appeals, the Director of First-year Composition replaces the Department Head of English in the appeals procedure, in accordance with the English Department bylaws. See Section II, "Appeals at the Department Level." Once a ruling on the grade appeal has been made, if either the student or instructor wants to take the appeal further, the appeal will be conducted according to the guidelines set out in Section III, "Appeals at the College Level."

Before appealing a grade, students should be aware of the following conditions established by the Franklin College Bylaws:

1. A student may appeal a grade if, and only if, he or she is able to demonstrate that the grade was based on factors other than a fair assessment of the student's academic performance in the course.

2. The standards by which grades are assigned, the number and relative weight of assignments on which grades are based, and decisions to allow students to make up or retake missed examinations or assignments, are not grounds for appeal.

Incompletes

The University assigns certain grades that are not computed in the grade point average. The Incomplete ("I") is one of these. It indicates that students have completed almost all of the course work satisfactorily but are unable to meet the full requirements of the course for reasons beyond their control.

When assigning Incompletes, instructors will explain in writing what students must do to finish the course. Students who receive Incompletes may have no longer than three semesters to complete all remaining work satisfactorily. Instructors can require that students complete work in a shorter period of time. If an "I" is not removed after three terms (including summer session), it changes to an "F." Incompletes are assigned sparingly and at the discretion of the instructor and the Director of the First-year Composition Program when a small amount of essential work remains. An "I" is never assigned prior to mid-semester or for the purpose of allowing students to repeat courses.

General Grading Weights

The meaning of grades is defined generally in the undergraduate version of the *University of Georgia Bulletin*: http://www.bulletin.uga.edu/.

The meaning of grades according to the First-year Composition Program and the Program Grading Rubric is defined as follows:

C	Competent / Credible / Complete	(70-79)
B	Skillful / Persuasive	(80-89)
A	Distinctive	(90-100)
D	Ineffective	(60-69)
F	Extremely Ineffective	(<60)
WF	Withdrew, failing	
WP	Withdrew, passing	

See the discussion of the FYC Grading Rubric below for more information about grading procedures.

Plus/Minus Grading

Plus and minus grades are assigned only to a student's final average for the course. For the final course grade in First-year Composition, the numerical range for each plus/minus grade is as follows:

A	4.0	(92-100)
A-	3.7	(90-91)
B+	3.3	(88-89)
B	3.0	(82-87)
B-	2.7	(80-81)
C+	2.3	(78-79)
C	2.0	(70-77)
C-	1.7	(68-69)
D	1.0	(60-67)
F	0.0	(<60)

CHAPTER FOUR

Using <emma>™
in the First-year Composition Program

A Brief Introduction to <emma>™

All students in First-year Composition (FYC) at UGA use the program's open-source, digital learning space, <emma>™.

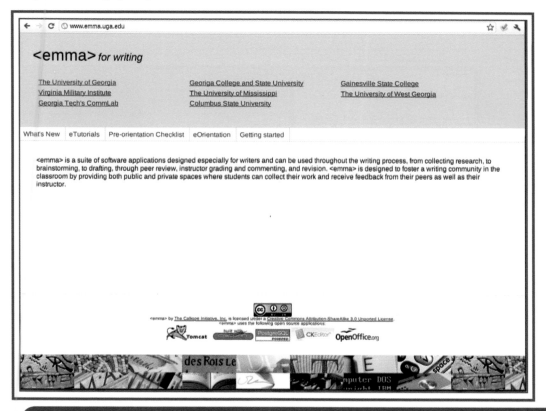

The <emma>™ Home Page

Designed especially for students and instructors, <emma>™ can be used throughout the composition process, from collecting research, brainstorming, and drafting through peer review, revision, and instructor grading and commenting. <emma>™ collects and organizes many of the tools useful for multimodal composition within an environment that is designed to foster a classroom learning community by providing both public and private spaces where students can collect their work and receive feedback from their peers and instructor.

For example, the Notes tool provides a private space where students can generate ideas and collect and begin organizing their notes and information about their sources. When you are ready to begin the drafting process, use the Notes tool to generate an outline from your research notes, including a preliminary Works Cited list. Then copy-and-paste your draft text into a document created using a word processor such as OpenOffice or save it as a new eDocument. Students can make these drafts available to the class for peer review or maintain them as private documents viewable only by themselves or their instructor.

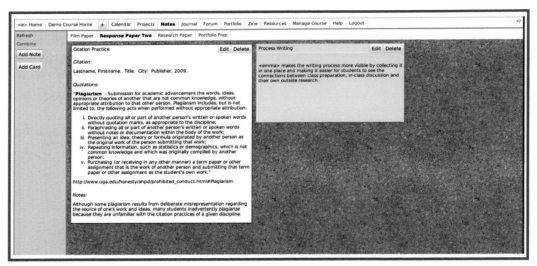

The Notes and Research Space

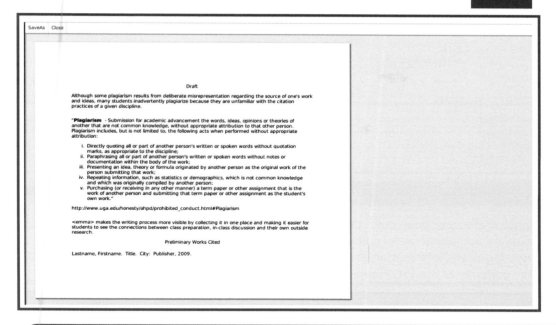

SaveAs   Close

Draft

Although some plagiarism results from deliberate misrepresentation regarding the source of one's work and ideas, many students inadvertently plagiarize because they are unfamiliar with the citation practices of a given discipline.

"**Plagiarism** - Submission for academic advancement the words, ideas, opinions or theories of another that are not common knowledge, without appropriate attribution to that other person. Plagiarism includes, but is not limited to, the following acts when performed without appropriate attribution:

   i. Directly quoting all or part of another person's written or spoken words without quotation marks, as appropriate to the discipline;
   ii. Paraphrasing all or part of another person's written or spoken words without notes or documentation within the body of the work;
   iii. Presenting an idea, theory or formula originated by another person as the original work of the person submitting that work;
   iv. Repeating information, such as statistics or demographics, which is not common knowledge and which was originally compiled by another person;
   v. Purchasing (or receiving in any other manner) a term paper or other assignment that is the work of another person and submitting that term paper or other assignment as the student's own work."

http://www.uga.edu/honesty/ahpd/prohibited_conduct.html#Plagiarism

<emma> makes the writing process more visible by collecting it in one place and making it easier for students to see the connections between class preparation, in-class discussion and their own outside research.

Preliminary Works Cited

Lastname, Firstname. Title. City: Publisher, 2009.

From Notes to Draft

The Comment function operates as an asynchronous chat and offers peers and instructors the opportunity to engage in an ongoing discussion of a draft-in-progress. For more focused peer and instructor review, students and instructors can use word-processor templates to integrate feedback offline and then upload the reviewed draft.

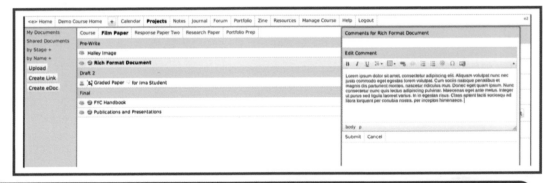

Draft with Online Comments

Once drafts have been peer and/or instructor reviewed and uploaded, <emma>™ displays additional useful content, such as information drawn from *The St. Martin's Handbook* and information about the relationship between instructor comments and the contents of the FYC Program Grading Rubric.

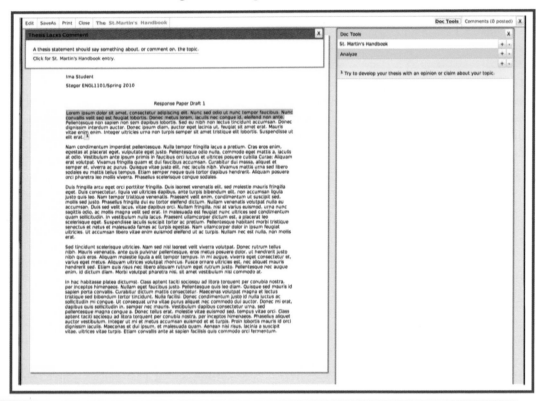

The Completed Document, with Helpful Information

The Journal tool offers students a private, informal space in which they can begin the writing process by reflecting on class readings and discussion. Journal entries are viewable only by the student and the instructor. Some classes also use the private Journal as a space for students to write reflections on their readings, drafts, and graded essays.

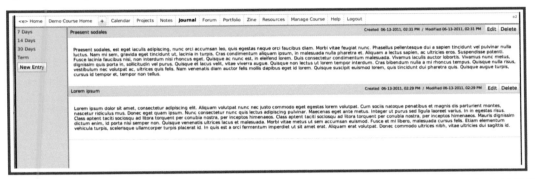

The <emma>™ Journal

The Forum tool is a public writing space where instructors and students can exchange ideas about readings, class discussions, and the composition process. Some classes also use the Forum as a convenient space for collective peer review; here, students can comment not only on essay drafts, but also on each other's comments. Forum postings are viewable by everyone enrolled in the class.

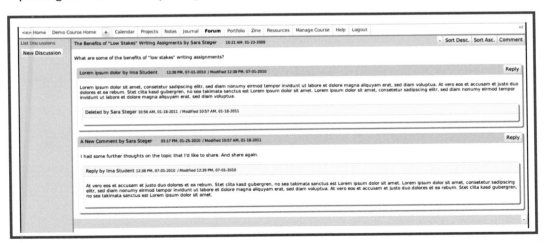

The Forum Space in <emma>™

For your final assignment in the course portfolio, you will collect exhibits of your work and reflections upon the composition process and other activities in your classroom learning community for your <emma>™ electronic portfolio. (See below for more information about the ePortfolio.)

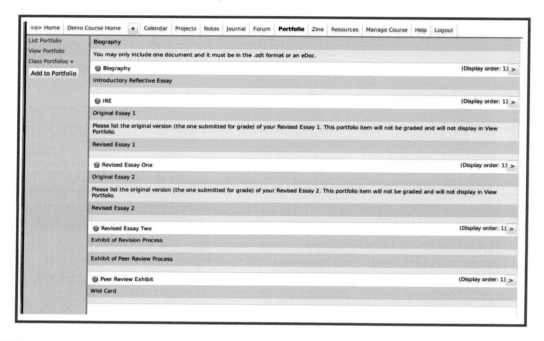

Your <emma>™ ePortfolio

Where the Portfolio provides a space for individual students to display their best work, plus specific skill sets that you have built up over the semester, class Zines offer collaborative workspaces that showcase the abilities of the class as a whole.

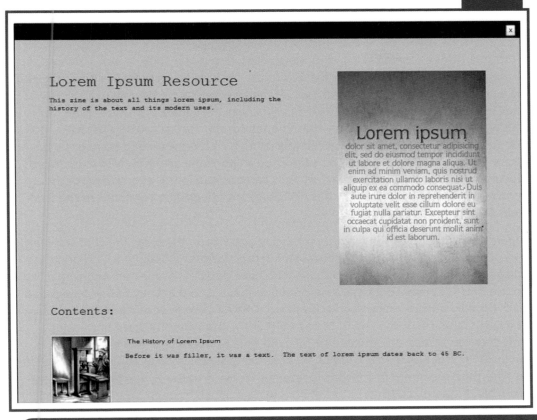

Lorem Ipsum Resource

This zine is about all things lorem ipsum, including the history of the text and its modern uses.

Lorem ipsum

dolor sit amet, consectetur adipisicing elit, sed do eiusmod tempor incididunt ut labore et dolore magna aliqua. Ut enim ad minim veniam, quis nostrud exercitation ullamco laboris nisi ut aliquip ex ea commodo consequat. Duis aute irure dolor in reprehenderit in voluptate velit esse cillum dolore eu fugiat nulla pariatur. Excepteur sint occaecat cupidatat non proident, sunt in culpa qui officia deserunt mollit anim id est laborum.

Contents:

The History of Lorem Ipsum

Before it was filler, it was a text. The text of lorem ipsum dates back to 45 BC.

A Class Zine Showcases the Skills of the <emma>™ Writing Community

Now, some technical information: Because FYC at UGA is interested in fostering an open and accessible learning community, <emma>™ uses the ODF standard, which has been adopted by the International Standards Organization (ISO) and the Organization for the Advancement of Structured Information Standards (OASIS). Unlike files saved in proprietary formats—such as .doc, .wpd, or the newer .docx—that can be created and accessed only by using relatively expensive word processing software (e.g., Microsoft Word or Corel WordPerfect), .odt files can be created and accessed using a number of free software applications.

In addition, because <emma>™ has been designed as a multimodal composition platform, it accepts MP3, JPEG, and PDF files, as well as ODF files containing multimedia elements such as images and hyperlinks. As long as they do not exceed the 4MB size limit, you can upload and access files in these additional multimedia formats. Depending upon the file format and the browser you are using, these files may be accessed within the browser and <emma>™ or you may need to download them.

<emma>™ does accept files in .doc, .docx., .ppt, and .pptx. They cannot, however, be displayed in the browser. Files in these formats can only be downloaded and accessed using the proprietary software with which they were created. Your instructor may or may not accept assignments in these formats over the course of the semester. **For the final portfolio, however, only files in open formats (eDocs, ODF, PDF, MP3, JPEG, SWF, FLV), which are generally accessible using a web browser and standard plug-ins or system software, should be submitted as portfolio artifacts. Microsoft Word documents (.doc or .docx format) will not be accepted in the ePortfolio. For more information, see the chapter in this *FYC Guide* on "Electronic Portfolios in the First-year Composition Program."**

OpenOffice, an open-source word processing application that uses the ODF standard, has been installed on all of the computers in the <emma>™ Lab (Park 117) and the Miller Learning Center (MLC). Students who have personal computers and would like to use them to create documents will need to make sure that they have downloaded and installed a word processor, such as OpenOffice (www.openoffice.org), that uses the ODF standard, or they need to ensure that their proprietary word processing software can access and create ODF files. **All final drafts of ODF files created for inclusion in the portfolio should be created using OpenOffice or converted to PDF to ensure that document formatting is retained in the browser to the greatest extent possible.** Students and instructors should remain aware, though, that the conversion from ODF to XHTML may occasionally result in minor formatting changes and make allowances for them. Students can get help with personal word processing solutions in the <emma>™ Lab.

In addition to using ODF-compliant word-processing software, students should use one of the following browsers to access <emma>™: Mozilla Firefox, Google Chrome, or Apple Safari. Like OpenOffice, Firefox has been installed on all of the computers in the <emma>™ Lab and the Miller Learning Center (MLC). Firefox, Chrome and Safari are all freely available for download from the web (www.mozilla.org, www.google.com/chrome/, and www.apple.com/safari/). Students can get help with downloading and installing these programs on their personal computers from the <emma>™ Lab.

To get an <emma>™ account, you can call up the <emma>™ homepage (www.emma.uga.edu) in an <emma>™-compatible browser and select "The University of Georgia." Then you should click on "Create Account" and <emma>™ will walk you through all of the steps necessary to create an account. Once you have an <emma>™ account, you can logon and enroll in a class from your personal <emma>™ homepage by clicking on "Enroll" in the left-hand toolbar.

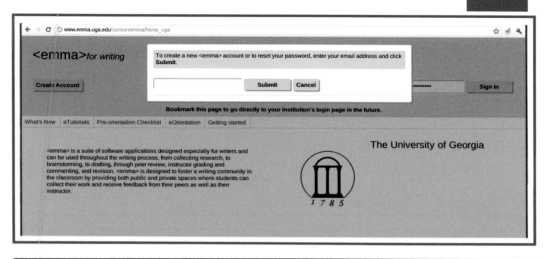

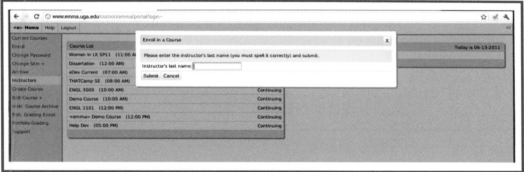

Creating your <emma>™ Account and Enrolling in a Course

From your <emma>™ homepage, you can also change the look and feel of <emma>™ by using the "Change Skin" feature and change your password from the default password generated when you created your account to something you will remember more easily. The homepage also provides notices and updates of upcoming events and assignments for all of the classes in which your instructor is using <emma>™.

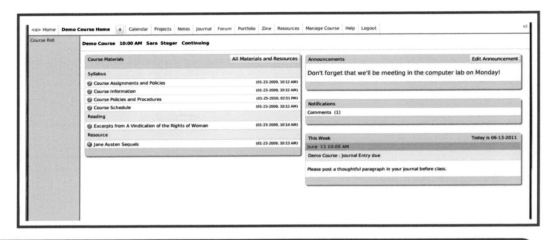

Once you are enrolled in a course, you can access your class by clicking on the name of the class on the <emma>™ homepage, which will take you to Course Home. Course Home gives you a quick snapshot of upcoming events for the week and a Class Roll where students can find instructor and peer e-mail addresses.

From anywhere in an <emma>™ course students can access course materials such as the syllabus, writing assignments, readings, handouts, and *The St. Martin's Handbook* by clicking on Resources on the top navigation menu.

<emma>™ organizes writing assignments into Projects. Instructors can associate readings, handouts and other resources with these Projects. By selecting Projects from the navigation bar at the top of the screen, students can access all of their own work related to that Project. This is also how students can find the work that their peers have made accessible for peer review.

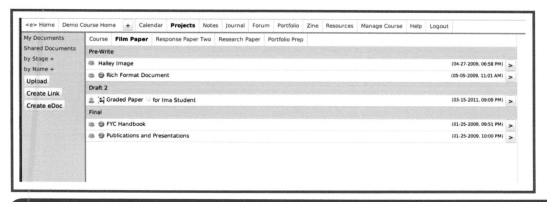

<emma>™ Organizes your Work According to Projects for the Course

The navigation bar also provides students with access to the <emma>™ Calendar, their Notes, the Journal, the Forum, class Zines, and the Portfolio. Instructors can use the Calendar to notify students of daily assignments, important due dates, and other events.

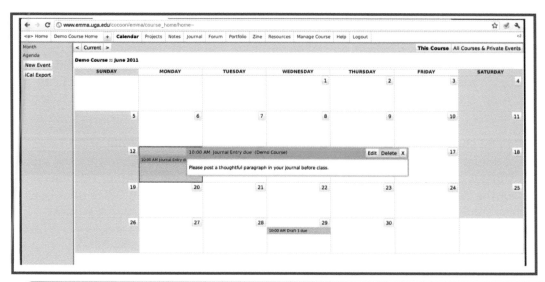

<emma>™ Helps You Keep Track of Assignments and Due Dates

...as been a quick tour of \<emma\> ™. You will learn more during your \<emma\> ™ ...tation and as you use \<emma\> ™ throughout the semester. You can also find more comprehensive information in the \<emma\> ™ Help documentation, and get assistance with using \<emma\> ™ from the \<emma\> ™ Support Team in the \<emma\> ™ Lab.

> The \<emma\> ™ Lab, where you can bring any of your \<emma\> ™ questions and problems, is in
>
> **Park Hall 117.**

\<emma\> ™ Lab and Support Team (Frogs)

First-year Composition students are encouraged to take advantage of the \<emma\> ™ Lab in Park 117. There, on any week day during regular business hours, you will find at least one member of the \<emma\> ™ support staff to answer any questions you may have about your \<emma\> ™ account and about the process of using \<emma\> ™. An appointment does not have to be made to use the \<emma\> ™ Lab; just drop in when the lab is open at a time most convenient for you.

The \<emma\> ™ Lab is staffed by First-year Composition teachers who use \<emma\> ™ in their classrooms and who often lead \<emma\> ™ orientations at the beginning of the semester and administer course and instructor evaluations near the end of the semester. Generically, individuals on the \<emma\> ™ support staff are referred to as "Frogs" – the reason being, historically, that technical support personnel "eat" "bugs." One can refer to the person occupying the desk at the front of the room as a "frog" without necessarily insulting him or her, provided that the tone used is not ironic.

Sign In: The \<emma\> ™ Lab has a sign-in sheet on the desk at the front of the room that students must sign before using the facilities. All one needs to know for the sign-in sheet is his or her name, his or her teacher's last name, and the time. This sheet is for the benefit of everyone, as it helps the First-year Composition Office track how many students are using the \<emma\> ™ Lab and when, and in so doing it ensures future funding and support for the lab.

Printing: There is also a printer available in the \<emma\> ™ Lab that First-year Composition students may use to print out materials necessary for their ENGL 1101, 1102, and 1102M classes. Students should be advised, however, that materials

printed for any other classes will not be made available to them after printing a[...]
will be recycled, instead. It is necessary to enforce this rule because the lab is fu[...]
through a special student fee, paid by all FYC students and only by FYC students, t[...]
allows use of these print resources for First-year Composition-related purposes only.

Lab Policies ~~& class room~~

- Out of respect for others and the work they are doing in the lab, please conduct cell phone conversations outside of the room;
- No food or drink in the lab;
- First-year Composition business takes precedence over any other for the lab computers. If you are not working on a project for your composition class, please allow students working with <emma>™ primary use of the lab's equipment.

Open Source Tools

Apart from Firefox, OpenOffice, and the usual office tools, a number of other open source tools have been added to the desktops of most of the lab computers. Three items of note are:

- Audacity, for sound editing/recording and mixing (be sure to bring your own headphones and microphone);
- Komposer, a web editor; and
- Gimp, a photoshop tool.

Recycling bins:

At times, the <emma>™ Lab can generate lots of paper. Please try to remember to recycle what you do not need in one of the bins at the front of the room.

Emma

1. Open Office   _(Robinson)_

Sign in to class

take the tutorials

3. Chrome

4 syllabus & Calendar

CHAPTER FIVE

Evaluation of Essays in the First-year Composition Program

5

What Do Teachers Want?

Because all writing, no matter how personal, attempts to communicate with some audience, writing is a social art. And all writers—whether students writing to develop their skills, amateurs writing to satisfy personal ambition, or professionals writing to support themselves—need to get some reaction to their writing. One form of reaction students get is from **peer review**. By critiquing one another's papers constructively in workshops, student writers gain immediate insight into the effectiveness of their argumentation and prose. Peer review is an important part of the assessment of students' work, for it allows students to get feedback from a range of real readers; the process of responding to other students' essays helps students to become good critics of their own, as well as of others', writing. This skill is important to much college work and is often cited by employers as being crucially important to the world of work. Because peer review is an important skill cultivated in First-year Composition, the capstone Electronic Portfolio includes a demonstration/discussion of the writer's Peer Review process. Students also receive comments and other feedback on some drafts and on graded essays from their First-year Composition teachers; this feedback, along with peer review commentary, is important to the job of revising graded essays for inclusion in the Electronic Portfolio.

How teachers grade an essay should interest all students. First, they should understand that no exact correlation exists between the number of marks, or even comments, on a paper and the grade that paper receives. An essay does not begin as a "100" and then lose points as the teacher finds mistakes. Although errors can seriously damage the overall effectiveness of a piece of writing, to write well students must do more than merely rid papers of grammatical and mechanical errors. Effective communication depends primarily on rhetorical concerns; in other words, how effectively does the writing assignment being evaluated meet the needs of a particular audience and accomplish a particular purpose?

To ensure consistency and good communication across the Program, all FYC classes use a common Program Grading Rubric, designed by a volunteer committee of teachers, which explains in greater detail our criteria for different grades. There are four basic categories: Competent/Credible/Complete, which describes essays that are satisfactory and passing and therefore fall into the "C" range; Skillful/Persuasive, which describes essays that are well above average—clearly superior to competent essays—and fall into the "B" range; Distinctive, which describes essays that stand out from even very competent essays in a singular or important way and therefore fall into the "A" range; Ineffective, which describes essays that, for different reasons, do not meet the basic criteria for competency.

Teachers and peers will offer comments and feedback to help you improve your work during successive stages of the drafting process. But when your instructor grades the final draft of your essay, she or he will decide, first of all, which of the four categories the essay falls into, using the particular criteria listed under each category for guidance. If your essay has Unity, Evidence and Development, and follows basic rules for Presentation and Design, it has earned a C. If in addition, your essay also has Coherence and Audience Awareness, you have entered the "B" range, and so forth. Once the instructor has commented on your work and determined the general category into which your essay falls, he or she will then decide holistically what place in the given point spectrum your essay falls. For instance, if the essay has Unity, Evidence, Presentation/Design, and Coherence, but lacks a good sense of audience, the instructor may determine that the essay falls toward the lower end of the Skillful/Persuasive spectrum (80-89 points): in such a case, your essay might earn an 82 or 83. If your essay has, in addition to the qualities detailed above, a strong personal voice that clearly demonstrated Audience Awareness through its ability to communicate with "real people," the essay might earn an 87 or 88.

Of course, there is no exact mathematical formula for determining grades. For instance, it is always possible that an essay that contains a few grammatical errors (Presentation/Design) or changes direction at one point (Unity) excels so clearly in more advanced criteria – say, a sense of Voice or excellent transitions from one idea to another – that the instructor decides it really should earn a B. In general, though, students should expect to satisfy all of the criteria for the Competent/Credible/Complete category in order to receive a passing grade.

The FYC Grading Rubric gives both students and teachers a common vocabulary for talking about writing quality and a set of important criteria for evaluating essays that are submitted for a grade during the semester and also those revised essays that are submitted in the capstone electronic portfolio. Some instructors use a special template in <emma> that links comments not only to criteria of the Grading Rubric (which helps students to understand their grades), but also to sections of *The St. Martin's Handbook* relevant to each criterion (which helps students to improve their writing). Students can also use the Rubric to assess the progress of their own essays as they move through the drafting process. Finally, as the Rubric indicates, teachers may include special requirements that affect students' final grades, adding or subtracting points based on those special, stated requirements. If you excel in these extra requirements or fail to meet them, your grade may be raised or lowered accordingly.

What Grades on Essays Mean

In more specific numerical terms, the meaning of grades is defined by the undergraduate version of the University of Georgia Bulletin: http://www.bulletin.uga.edu/. The meaning of grades according to the First-year Composition Program and grading rubric is defined as follows:

C	Competent / Credible / Complete	(70-79)
B	Skillful / Persuasive	(80-89)
A	Distinctive	(90-100)
D	Ineffective	(60-69)
F	Extremely Ineffective	(<60)
WF	Withdrew, failing	
WP	Withdrew, passing	

Plus/Minus Grading

Plus and minus grades are assigned only to a student's final average for the course. For the final course grade, the numerical range for each plus/minus grade is as follows:

A	4.0	(92-100)
A-	3.7	(90-91)
B+	3.3	(88-89)
B	3.0	(82-87)
B-	2.7	(80-81)
C+	2.3	(78-79)
C	2.0	(70-77)
C-	1.7	(68-69)
D	1.0	(60-67)
F	0.0	(<60)

ading Rubric

Here is the actual rubric that your teacher will use when evaluating your essays and often will encourage you to use when critiquing your peers' essays and making judgments about your own work.

Student's Name_____   Teacher _____

Paper #____   Special Assignment Requirements: _____

"Enter a pertinent quote here." (Teachers can self-select)

Conference_____

Writing Center_____

_____ **Competent/Credible/Complete**
If you meet these first three standards, you are writing <u>competently</u> and you will earn a grade of "C." (70-79)

1. **Unity**
   - Contains a center of gravity, a unifying and controlling purpose, a thesis or claim, which is maintained throughout the paper.
   - Organizes writing around a thesis or according to the organizational requirements of the particular assignment (e.g., summary, narrative, argument, analysis, description, etc.)
2. **Evidence/Development**
   - Develops appropriate, logical, and relevant supporting detail and/or evidence.
   - Includes more specific, concrete evidence (or details) than opinion or abstract, general commentary.
3. **Presentation and Design**
   - Follows SMH guidelines for Standard English grammar, punctuation, usage, and documentation.
   - Meets your teacher's (or the MLA's) and the First-year Composition program's requirements for <u>length</u> and/or format.

_____ **Skillful/Persuasive**
If you meet all of the competency standards above and, in addition, achieve coherence and exhibit audience awareness, you are writing <u>skillfully</u> and you will earn a grade of "B." (80-89)

4. **Coherence**
   - Uses words and sentences, rhythm and phrasing, variations and transitions, concreteness and specificity to *reveal and emphasize the relationship* between evidence and thesis.
   - Explains how, why, or in what way the evidence/detail provided supports the claim/ point /thesis/topic ideas.
   - Incorporates evidence from outside sources smoothly, appropriately, and responsibly.
5. **Audience Awareness**
   - Demonstrates a sense that the writer knows what s/he's doing and is addressing real people.
   - Reflects a respect for values that influence ethos (e.g., common ground, trustworthiness, careful research).

_____ **Distinctive**
If you meet all of the competency standards, achieve coherence and exhibit audience awareness, and, in addition, demonstrate a mastery of one or more features of superior writing, you are writing <u>distinctively</u> and you will earn a grade of "A." (90-100)

6. **Distinction**
   - Your writing stands out because of one or more of the following characteristics: complexity, originality, seamless coherence, extraordinary control, sophistication in thought, recognizable voice, compelling purpose, imagination, insight, thoroughness, and/or depth.

Essay Grade _____ **+/- Points for special assignment requirements** _____ = | **Final Grade** |

_____ **Ineffective**
If your paper does not meet competency standards, either because you have minor problems in all three competence areas (1-3 above) or major problems in one or two competence areas, you will earn a grade of "D" (60-69) or "F" (<60), and you should schedule a <u>conference</u> with your teacher.

Using the First-year Composition Grading Rubric's Vocabulary

We use the FYC Grading Rubric throughout our First-year Composition program because it helps teachers, tutors, students, and sometimes advisors, parents, and administrators to understand what our program values and looks for in student writing. Many teachers use an electronic version of this rubric and mark essays with coded electronic tags and inserted comments, while other teachers clip or staple a paper copy of the rubric, along with their handwritten notes, directly to student papers. Whether paper or electronic — whichever form of the rubric they use — teachers depend on the standard Rubric's language to guide their evaluation of student papers, while students must depend to some degree on the Rubric's language to understand their teachers' comments. Finally, the Rubric's common vocabulary helps students comment on one another's work and to make judgments about their own essays. The Rubric helps to keep all parties on the same page!

In order to help students (and teachers) use the Rubric most effectively, here we discuss some of the key terms:

Competent/Credible/Complete

In order to receive a passing and satisfactory grade of "C," an essay needs to meet the three principal criteria of Unity, Evidence/Development, and Presentation and Design.

1. Unity = Staying on topic and providing structure

"Contains a center of gravity, a unifying and controlling purpose, a thesis or claim, which is maintained throughout the paper."

First-year compositions can be organized in many different ways. Papers may have an implicit or explicit thesis, or they may simply have a unifying purpose or theme. In any unified paper, however, **every sentence and every word will contribute in some way towards the exposition and development of the "main" idea**.

Notice, too, that at the level of Competency "unity" does not require a particularly complex, clever, or imaginative thesis, nor does unity require strong coherence. For example, if my thesis were "cats are annoying," unity would only require that every sentence be somehow relevant to the "topic" (i.e., "cats") and the "comment" (i.e., "are annoying"), the two elements that *The St. Martin's Handbook* defines as central to a thesis. Teachers may need to read between the lines a bit in evaluating a paper for unity; peer review can also provide useful feedback to writers about the unity of their essays. For instance, sometimes an apparently unrelated comment, such as "Cats often have long, fluffy fur," may need just a word or two (perhaps a word or two about shedding, allergies and long, fluffy fur on couches!) to firmly demonstrate unity.

organizes writing around a thesis or according to the organizational requirements of the particular assignment (e.g., summary, narrative, argument, analysis, description, etc.)"

organize writing around a thesis" or **other central point** means that the essay reveals, under examination, **an overall organizational plan or strategy**. Could this essay be outlined? Does it have a definite beginning, middle, and end? A clearly organized essay might use logical, spatial, chronological, or even associational order—but the strategy will suit the topic and the purpose of the paper.

2. Evidence/Development = Providing support (examples, details, or specifics)

"Develops appropriate, logical, and relevant supporting detail and/or evidence."

This criterion asks you to note whether the writer uses examples and/or other evidence to support his/her argument, position, or idea and whether that evidence is fairly used, accurate, and relevant. Depending on the kind of essay you have been assigned, good evidence may include anecdotes, images, descriptions, and dialogue or primary and secondary sources, graphs, and charts; typically, evidence will include quotations from a variety of sources—often the texts read in class. You are evaluating the **quality of evidence** and sources here. Did the writer use the evidence accurately and fairly? Or to give another example, was the scene described with concrete details?

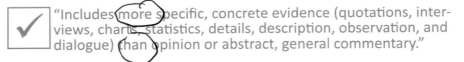
"Includes more specific, concrete evidence (quotations, interviews, charts, statistics, details, description, observation, and dialogue) than opinion or abstract, general commentary."

This criterion asks you to gauge **quantity of evidence**. Has the writer spent most of the essay making general statements and assertions about the topic? Or, instead, has he/she used most of his/her words and sentences to clarify and define the argument, giving examples and explaining connections to assertions? How many opinion statements are there versus how many examples/quotations/details? Typically, you would hope to find a good deal more evidence than opinion. On the other hand, does the writer string together many quotations and facts into lists or very lengthy quoted passages? Is there **too much** unincorporated and unexplained evidence?

3. Presentation and Design = Correctness and formatting issues

"Follows guidelines for standard English grammar, punctuation, usage, and documentation."

To meet this criterion, here is a general rule of thumb: To pass at the level of Competency, a paper should contain 2 or fewer major errors + 4 or fewer minor errors/250-

word page or 8 or fewer minor errors/250-word page. All the major errors have to do with either sentence boundary recognition or Standard English grammar issues. For our purposes, the major errors are:

- Comma Splice
- Fragment
- Fused Sentence
- Subject/Verb Agreement
- Pronoun/Antecedent Agreement

All other errors are considered minor errors. If a student's paper has more errors than the standard described above, the paper is not meeting competency guidelines.

Remember, however, that this standard is just a guideline. Simply lacking a large number of errors does not necessarily make an essay "Competent" or passing. As we point out in the Introduction to this section: "An essay does not begin as a '100' and then lose points as the teacher finds mistakes."

 "Meets your teacher's (or the MLA's) and the First-year Composition Program's requirements for length and/or format."

The standard format and documentation requirements for First-year Composition follow those for MLA formatting. Teachers may have special requirements, which could include things like specialized or alternative style sheets, images, graphs, particular fonts, minimum word counts, bibliographies, appendices, notes, abstracts, etc.

EXAMPLE:

Here is an excerpt from Kaitlyn Downs's 2010-2011 Barnett Award Essay showing how a student working at the Distinctive level excels in all three Competency requirements. The opening paragraph of Kaitlyn's essay establishes her thesis — that "Shakespeare uses the story of Christopher Sly's taming and its counterpart, Kate's taming, to show that appearance becomes reality"—while the subsequent paragraphs printed here analyze the Induction of *The Taming of the Shrew* to support that point. Kaitlyn discusses two different characters in the course of her essay, but the essay has unity because she focuses the discussion of them specifically in terms of the themes of identity and appearance versus reality; this consistent focus gives her essay a "center of gravity." The essay also makes excellent use of evidence from both primary and secondary sources, alternating paraphrase and summary with direct quotation; note as well that the supporting quotations do not overwhelm Kaitlyn's prose, but are integrated into her own sentences to establish logical support for her own points. In the following sentence, for instance, you can see that Kaitlyn immediately follows her textual evidence with an explanation of its significance: "Not only does Sly state his belief in his nobility, but he also exhibits changes in his language, *demonstrating the sincerity of his personality change*." (See more on this point in the discussion of the Skillful/Persuasive category.) Explaining the evidence gives Kaitlyn's essay a strong sense of argumentative development. Additionally, the essay uses correctly MLA conventions for citation of plays and critical articles.

In the excerpt, all portions related to the essay's **thesis** and **center of gravity** are marked in **green**, while **evidence** is marked in **purple**.

If something walks like a duck, quacks like a duck, and acts like a duck, is it a duck? Probably, but what if this "duck" is really just a confused chicken? At this point, the question of identity comes into play. Is the chicken then considered a duck because its actions all point towards that of the distinctive aquatic bird? Or does the chicken's actual reality as a chicken, its feathery DNA, matter more in this discussion? Identity in *The Taming of the Shrew* acts the same way. Highlighting the nature of identity, Shakespeare uses the story of Christopher Sly's taming and its counterpart, Kate's taming, *to show that appearance becomes reality*. Ultimately, the characters in *The Taming of the Shrew* blur the lines between reality and illusion, making them one and the same.

In the beginning of the play, the small part of dialogue concerning Christopher Sly shows the phenomenon of illusion becoming reality. A rich lord abducts Sly, a drunken beggar, and plays a trick on him: "What think you, if he were . . . wrapped in sweet clothes, rings put upon his fingers, a most delicious banquet by his bed . . . Would not the beggar then forget himself?" (Shakespeare, *Taming of the Shrew*, Ind. 1.33-37). When Sly awakens in an unfamiliar setting, he questions the truth of his predicament, but eventually, he wholeheartedly accepts the illusion that "[he is] a lord indeed, and not a tinker nor Christopher Sly" (Ind. 2.68-69). Because Sly sees that he possesses all the characteristics of a lord — fine clothes, dedicated servants, a noble "wife" — he immediately accepts the façade.

When he accepts his pseudo-nobility, Sly's paradigm of his own reality shifts completely. He notices that he possesses all the characteristics of a lord and adjusts his own identity accordingly: he becomes the lord. Initially, the changes in Sly are merely superficial; he gains obedient servants, nice clothes, and delicious food. Nothing about his personality should change, but it does. Not only does Sly state his belief in his nobility, but he also exhibits changes in his language demonstrating the sincerity of his personality change. Critic Joseph Tate cites the fact that Sly's form of speaking changes from prose, indicating a peasant, to blank verse, traditionally a form of speech used by poets and playwrights for aristocratic speech (106). Christopher Sly's "[rise] to verse and into nobility," indicates that a real change occurs in Sly's perception of himself and, therefore, in his actual identity (106).

Excerpted from: "Character Identity in *The Taming of the Shrew*"
Student: Kaitlyn Downs
Teacher: Beth Kozinsky (ENGL 1102)

Skillful/Persuasive

In order to reach the level of a "Skillful/Persuasive" paper, an argument must have two additional qualities: Coherence and Audience Awareness

4. Coherence = The "Flow"

> ✓ "Uses words and sentences, rhythm and phrasing, variations and transitions, concreteness and specificity to reveal and emphasize the relationship between evidence and thesis."

In general, while students can achieve unity by creating a strong thesis and staying on topic, they create coherence by focusing their reader's attention on the *relationship* between thesis and evidence (or theme and detail). Creating Coherence is about **controlling emphasis**.

wordiness + Redundancy   *paragraph*

Students may use diction to emphasize the thesis-to-evidence connections by choosing words carefully, by repeating key words and phrases, by avoiding the repetition of unimportant words and phrases, and by using transitional phrases accurately. Writers can also use syntax, that is, sentence structure, to direct emphasis by varying sentence structures, by using syntactical effects such as parallelism and antithesis, or by simply changing sentence length or reversing normal Subject-Verb-Object sentence patterns. In evaluating coherence, you can ask these questions: has the writer used syntax and diction to create links between his or her thoughts? Does the writer use transitional phrases and words frequently and accurately to help the reader move from sentence to sentence and from paragraph to paragraph? Does the writer's use of repetition, parallelism, figures of speech, and rhythm help to emphasize main points, or does the writer's choice of diction and syntax distract the reader from the main ideas?

how happened why so what

Exp

> ✓ "Explains how, why, or in what way the evidence/detail supports a point/claim/thesis/topic ideas."

Writers need to include **explanations**. In fact, writers usually need to explain why each detail or item of support has been included in an essay. It is a rare bit of evidence that is so clear that it speaks for itself. Coherence develops as writers **explain how** each part of their arguments' evidence provides support for their theses.

> ✓ "Incorporates evidence from outside sources smoothly, appropriately, and responsibly."

Later

The writer will consistently incorporate quotations and references to other outside sources into her own sentences. Coherent writers move often between paraphrasing, summarizing, and brief selected quotations from different sources. Few, if any, quotations will be left "hanging"—that is, standing alone in separate sentences; instead, they will be embedded in the writer's own sentences, usually with explanatory re-marks linking the quotations to the topic or thesis. Lengthy quotations, serial quota-tions, or long summaries rarely occur in a "Skillful" writer's essay. Both examples below offer good examples of smoothly inserted quotations and responsible citation practices.

EXAMPLE:

The first example below comes from Revised Essay 1 in Victoria Moreira's Moran Award-winning English 1102M portfolio. Entitled "A Struggle between Warring Worlds," the essay analyzes how "two clashing worlds emerge" in each of two differ-ent multicultural poems. Here, the author is discussing Nora Naranjo-Morse's "Mud Woman's First Encounter with the World of Money and Business."

Transition words, phrases, and clauses are marked in blue. Notice as well the great variety in Victoria's sentence structure and the smooth way in which she incorporates relevant quotations into her own sentences. (If you remove mentally the quotation marks from a sentence that contains a citation from the poem, the sentence will make perfect grammatical sense; try it!) You can also see a good example of how to incorporate quotations in Kaitlyn Downs's essay, part of which is reprinted above.

In "Mud Woman," the two worlds of the confusing city life and the familiar reservation life collide, leaving Mud Woman vulnerable. Mud Woman, who enters this new business-world, is ready to share a part of herself with it, looking to start anew and to start her exploration of the world she belongs to. When she arrives at the gallery to start her journey into the business world, immediately the "center of what [she] knew to be real / was shifting with each moment" (Naranjo-Morse lines 28-29). The two worlds begin to collide. The gallery-owner, whom Mud Woman first meets, represents the materialistic business world that cares only about the superficial and profit-able importance of a person when it comes to a business venture. Converse-ly, Mud Woman, in a genuine way through her mud figurines, represents the unique natural culture and traditions from her reservation life. The business world works in a way that Mud Woman does not understand. In an obtrusive manner, when introducing the rules of society to Mud Woman, the gallery owner arrogantly asks, "First of all dear, do you have a resume? You know, / something written that would identify you to the public" (lines 19-20). As the gallery owner asks Mud Woman about her resume, she plays by the rules of the business world; she only cares about how the public will respond to Mud Woman's artwork. The woman wants "traditional" Indian artwork to sell in her gallery because that is what is profitable—unlike the "strangely different" figurines that Mud Woman makes (line 43). The woman does not believe there is any chance of opportunity for *herself* in Mud Woman's work, yet she buys a few of her pieces because "if for some reason [Mud Woman] make[s] it big, / [she] can be the first to say, 'I discovered you' " (lines 48-49). The gallery owner is purely self-interested and motivated only by profit—ignoring all sense of Mud Woman's feelings. Before she knows it, Mud woman "exchanged her work for the / unexpectedly smaller sum that wholesale prices dictated" (lines 54-55). During the period of this exchange, Mud Woman has no voice—she passively allows the business world to take advantage of her and her artwork. The wholesale prices of the "traditional" Indian artwork that Mud Woman's work is categorized in automatically dictate the value of her work — Mud Woman's unique and careful labor with the way she "concern[ed] herself with the specific curves, bends and / idiosyncrasies, that made each piece her own" is pushed aside for a cheap buy by the business world (lines 4-5). Mud woman, betrayed by this foreign world, realizes that she does not belong to it.

Excerpted from: "A Struggle between Warring Worlds"
Student: Victoria Moreira
Instructor: Laura Weaver (ENGL 1102M)

EXAMPLE:

In the second example, from Deanna Stevens's English 1102M Barnett Award essay, you can see how the author is careful to explain the significance of her evidence. While the paragraph begins with a list of the symbols Joy Harjo uses in her poem "Hieroglyphic," Deanna quickly illustrates her thesis with a quotation from the poem, followed then by explanation of the symbols contained there. This is a fairly long quotation—longer than those in Kaitlyn's or Victoria's essays—but taking up that much space with a quotation is justified in this case because the quotation is followed by extensive discussion and because the essay talks about the line structure as well as the symbolism of Harjo's poem; in this instance, the visual evidence of the quotation helps to clarify some complicated points. In general, though, it's best to limit direct quotation to the specific words and phrases that you want to emphasize in your argument and to weave the quotations into your own sentences. You'll note as well that Deanna supports her thesis with evidence from both the poem itself and secondary sources, which gives extra power to her explanations. Deanna's extensive **explanation** of how and why evidence supports her thesis is highlighted in **green**.

In "Hieroglyphic," Harjo writes of a phoenix, skeleton horses, a crocodile, and a snake as she describes her spiritual experiences in the Egyptian room and spontaneously remembers a dream from her childhood. In realizing the correlation between present moment and memory as a spiritual revelation, Harjo attempts to describe the gravity of her realization through the use of verse and symbolic writing. In creating an atmosphere that welcomes the reader into a layering of consciousness, she writes in lines 44-50:

> be born on paper. It goes something like this: when the
>   mythic spiral of time
> turned its beaded head and understood what was going
>   on, it snapped. All
>
> these years I had been sleeping in the mind of the snake,
>   June. I have to tell
> this to someone.

The snake has been seen as a symbol of rebirth, self-reflexivity, and eternal cyclic change. In "Hieroglyphic," Harjo reflects on the timeline of her life as a serpentine entity that snaps at the moment of her realization. By weaving together these dream-like images that refer to folk tales and creation myths, she references Jung's abstract archetypes, seamlessly blended within the present moment and memory. In a review of Jung's principles of symbols in religious and unconscious archetypes, Carlsson addresses this type of revelation specifically, saying, "A man [or woman] dreams about a snake, and in Jungian theory, the snake is a symbol for something the unconscious is trying to say to the individual. What the unconscious wishes to communicate depends upon the state of the individual's inner condition" (38). Harjo introduces the concept of time as a snake in "Hieroglyphic"; she reflects upon the symbolic nature of the messages from her dream world. The reader is never more involved than in the moment of realization when Harjo puts together her memory and present experience and denies the reader any sense of linear time by combining both past and future in the present. Through myth, her most extensively used instrument, Harjo takes the reader "into the realm where anything is possible, where meaning is exploded" (Scarry 286).

> Excerpted from: "Considering the Physical and Symbolic in Joy Harjo's
> 'The Myth of Blackbirds' and 'Hieroglyphic'"
> Student: Deanna Stevens
> Instructor: Liz Vasconcelos-Hammock (ENGL 1102M)

5. Audience Awareness = Writing should speak to real readers

 "Demonstrates a sense that the writer knows what s/he's doing and is addressing real people."

Showing that a writer "knows what s/he's doing" means that the writer works to develop his or her credibility (ethos). He or she might mention and/or demonstrate particular knowledge or research concerning the topic, demonstrate comfort and familiarity with appropriate jargon or professional vocabularies, or simply use sound logic and clear reasoning in his or her discussion. Credibility can be, however, developed in many ways.

EXAMPLE:

In "Diary of a Facebook Convert," Thomas Parrott both establishes his credibility and creates a sense that he is talking to real people through the essay's personal voice, which is both entertaining and authoritative, and through humor. In the final paragraphs of his essay, you can see how Thomas uses prose style to create this distinctive voice and to communicate his ethos, which is at once professional and casual.

> Of course, these days I've left the military behind and moved on into a new stage of my life. The hair cut, the clothes, and the attitude all changed as I came to the University of Georgia, and the way I used social media changed, too. Part of it is role reversal, as I'm the one sending friends overseas the messages encouraging them to keep their chin up. My usage goes further than that, though: it's not about just keeping in touch with old friends anymore. Now it's about networking with new ones, making and maintaining the connections that are going to carry me through the college years and on into the rest of my life. As my life changes, my use of Facebook just changes too, leaving me convinced it's not going anywhere any time soon.
>
> Now that we've charted my course from an absolute social media skeptic to a Facebook true believer, I won't claim that I don't still see flaws in the progress of social media, or that I've bought into the whole scheme. I've seen it exacerbate too much drama and provoke too many arguments all by itself, not to mention the occasional violations of privacy and the like. In the end, though, it lets me keep in touch with friends and family scattered all across the country and even the world, and if nothing else, I'm grateful for that opportunity. Just don't get me started on Twitter, as I still can't quite take that sort of nonsense. At least, until my mother gets an account.

Excerpted from: "Diary of a Facebook Convert"
Student: Thomas Parrott
Instructor: Allison Lenhardt (ENGL 1101)

EXAMPLE:

Another example from an altogether different kind of essay can be found in the opening paragraph of Courtney Purvis's Revised Essay 1 in her Moran Award portfolio. Discussing the medical condition of schizophrenia, Courtney establishes her credibility with strong diction and citations from scientific research, but speaks directly to her readers ("Imagine being in a room . . .") to give schizophrenia a human face and elicit the readers' empathy. Precise use of medical and scientific terms also enhances Courtney's ethos.

" The Fortunate Unhappy"
A Potential Remedy for schizophrenia
Courtney Purvis

Imagine being in a room surrounded by empty faces of characters speaking with monotonous voices. You may understand the words they say, but you are still baffled by their meaning. Unable to make a connection with anyone, you feel despondent and lost. In reality, the menagerie of the unknown was just as normal as any daily interaction, but without the ability to read emotions. Schizophrenia is classified as a mental disorder that affects social behaviors and thought process. It is known to cause abnormal movements and psychosis in the form of paranoia and the occurrences of extreme hallucinations. The scenario in the room filled with ubiquitous confusion represents a symptom of schizophrenia that is constantly overlooked by the public and media: the inability to visually recognize emotions. Those suffering from schizophrenia are able to discern their own emotions, but cannot discern those of others, presenting a serious impediment in social and neurological development (Dryden-Edwards 1). People with schizophrenia are not indifferent to feeling; their ability to empathize is just greatly hindered. A possible solution to this social dilemma is a neuropeptide known as oxytocin, which is currently used to treat similar symptoms in autism (Marazziti 698). Unfortunately, the synthesized hormone has not been widely tested as a treatment for schizophrenia. Subsequently, the complete relation between schizophrenic behavior and oxytocin is yet unknown.

Excerpted from: "'The Fortunate Unhappy': A Potential Remedy for Schizophrenia"
Student: Courtney Purvis
Instructor: Sharon McCoy (ENGL1102)

 "Reflects a respect for values that influence ethos (e.g., common ground, trustworthiness, careful research)."

Respect for an audience and values can be shown at every level. Has the writer chosen an appropriate level of formality in his or her diction — avoiding the too formal for an audience of close friends, the too familiar with teachers or general audiences? Has the writer avoided unnecessary jargon or slang? Has the writer avoided sexist or racist language? Is the writer's choice of supporting examples and evidence appropriate, fairly used, relevant, and judiciously applied? Does the writer show a high level of integrity about facts and correctness at every level? Does the writer implicitly and explicitly show courtesy and good will towards readers whose opinions may differ? Does the writer acknowledge counter-arguments and other positions?

EXAMPLE:

Any of the award-winning essays published in the *FYC Guide* can be used to illustrate this criterion. For instance, the opening thesis paragraph of Kaitlyn Downs's essay on *The Taming of the Shrew* bases its authority on the author's use of logic to persuade the reader that her thesis is valid. Courtney Purvis's essay shows a respect for careful research, both in the science she studies and in her own scholarship. A slightly unusual example of an essay that shows respect for values that influence ethos comes from Brittany Scott's Peer Review Exhibit from her Moran Award portfolio for English 1101. Because in the Peer Review Exhibit, writers have to show how they are able to help another person without bragging too much about themselves, this can be a difficult piece to write. Through a clear narrative about her exchanges with classmate "August Mayhem," Brittany shows that she understands the rationale for peer review, which is rooted in a sense of cooperation and collaboration, a logical process of analysis and composition, plus close attention to information and subject matter. (You can see the illustrated version of Brittany's Peer Review Exhibit in the Moran Portfolio Awards section of this book.)

THE PHONE CALL

The conversation usually takes place for the same reason each time. I call her because while attempting to edit her first draft, I realized she had not uploaded it to Emma yet. When we get on the phone, I will ask her what she wants to write about and she will tell me her idea. For this particular example, she wanted to write an analytical essay on the cover of a VOGUE magazine. I was familiar with the magazine, so I could help her brainstorm. Also, August had a strong foundation of information in history and fashion. Therefore, a picture like the one to the right was of her comfort zone. By the end of the conversation, August and I had developed a descriptive purpose for her paper. In her essay, August was to explain how the image attracts readers and creates controversy regarding stereotypes.

> Excerpted from: "Sharing the Love"
> Student: Brittany Scott
> Instructor: Christy Desmet (ENGL 1101)

Distinctive

To earn the highly coveted grade of "A," a writer must go beyond basic criteria required for a competent essay, exceed the expectations for a skillful essay, and provide something else that gives the essay real "value added," sticks in the reader's memory, or catches her attention.

6. Distinction: A few words about distinction

 "Your writing stands out because of one or more of the following characteristics: complexity, originality, seamless coherence, extraordinary control, sophistication in thought, recognizable voice, compelling purpose, imagination, insight, thoroughness, and/or depth."

No single quality reveals distinction; that's why we've listed so many possibilities. A paper should meet standards in all five of the other criteria before it is considered for "Distinction." This does not mean students' papers must necessarily **excel** in all five criteria (although many will and most will excel in 3 or more criteria), but papers **should be average or better in every category and should not be deficient in any category** when being considered for Distinction.

The FYC Grading Rubric was designed by a volunteer team of instructors who carefully examined a range of essays, deciding what qualities papers at different grade levels shared in common. Based on their work, we now have a common vocabulary that students and teachers can use to understand how to succeed in First-year Composition.

CHAPTER SIX

Electronic Portfolios in the First-year Composition Program

6

o original Essays

The First-year Composition Electronic Portfolio

Every student who takes a First-year Composition course at the University of Georgia composes an electronic portfolio over the course of the semester. The ePortfolio gives students an opportunity to revise and polish their work—even after it has been evaluated for a grade during the semester—to showcase their work in a personalized context, to reflect on their writing and their writing processes, and, finally, to "publish" their work to a broader audience. The use of an electronic portfolio for all FYC classes means that students have an opportunity to raise their grades through steady *Typo* work and revision; but it also means that students need to schedule adequate time to do their very best work in the portfolio, as it counts for approximately 30% of their final grade.

Students develop portfolios throughout the semester using the First-year Composition Program's <emma>™ writing environment—adding, updating, and revising elements under teachers' directions and using the support available in the <emma>™ Lab in Park Hall 117. Students will also find that using feedback from their classmates in peer review sessions, both in and out of class, will make portfolio development a much more rewarding process.

The details of using <emma>™ to compose your ePortfolio will be described during Orientation sessions and during classes. In addition, individual teachers will make specific assignments for various parts of the portfolio. In broad outline, however, the essential seven components of our ePortfolios are consistent in every FYC course and are described briefly below:

Elements of the Portfolio

Front Page: Biography + Image

The biography or "bio" is a short introduction to you, the author of the portfolio. Your class or teacher may specify particular information to include in your bio, but, in general, the bio should act as an author's headnote and therefore is often around 300-500 words in length.

Images on your bio page are optional, but readers like them, so you should try to in-clude some image that is relevant. You can select a representative image (a windmill, a horse, or anything you can find on the Web—just remember to include a citation), or you can select an image of yourself. Think of it as a dust jacket image on the back of a book—how do you want to represent yourself? The goal of your Bio and Image page should be to establish a credible ethos.

> Note: The Bio MUST either be in ODT format or be constructed as an <emma>™ eDocument to display properly in your <emma>™ portfolio. We strongly recommend creating it using either OpenOffice or eDocs. You must also check carefully to make sure that the Biography displays properly, as this will provide portfolio readers with their first impression of you as a writer.

Introductory Reflective Essay

The most important element in your ePortfolio, the Introductory Reflective Essay provides a reader with an introduction and guide to the rest of your work. A strong IRE ties together all the exhibits in your portfolio; it helps you describe and reflect on your writing processes, with your exhibits providing the supporting evidence. The Re-flective Introduction is also the first item evaluators will read after they open your Bio page. Your teacher may provide you with a specific prompt or s/he may direct you to some specific portion of the FYC program sample prompt to help you get started. In your IRE, you might discuss how the various exhibits you have chosen for your portfo-lio reveal the way you have engaged with the goals of the course listed earlier in this FYC Guide and/or the FYC Grading Rubric's criteria. Some very successful portfolios have re-organized the author's work for the semester around a common theme that the writer sees in her or his own work. 750-1500 words is the average length for an IRE, although some of the Moran Award winners have written longer IRE's.

Two Revised Essays from the Course

You will include in your Electronic Portfolio two of the three graded papers you have written for the class, revised and polished and posted to the portfolio. They should be substantive and well-argued, carefully edited, error free, and completely, thoroughly, and correctly documented in MLA format.

> Note about the Revised Essays: We recommend a thorough revision for the Revised Essays exhibits in your Portfolio—not just a quick proofread-ing for surface errors. Could more evidence be developed, a new perspec-tive raised, for instance, a change in tone attempted, or a firmer line of reasoning followed?

> When choosing essays to put in your Electronic Portfolio, think about how they will work together to help make the portfolio a unified whole. Some students choose the essays which have received the highest grades, but

this is only one criterion. You may want to choose the essays you like the best, the ones you can improve the most, or the ones that fit best with your chosen theme.

Exhibit of Composing/Revision Process

This exhibit demonstrates your composing and revision process. Typically, students construct this document by copying and pasting the same or similar sections of a selected essay into a single document. You can then add commentary explaining the significance of the different versions, pointing out and explaining the changes you made through successive drafts. The Revision Exhibit gives you a chance to demonstrate not so much your best products for the semester, as the skill set that you have built up over the course. The trick is to make it easy for a reader to follow the process; the explanation is just as important as, or perhaps more important than, your chosen examples. This exhibit gives you a chance to reflect on your progress throughout the semester and to perform a self-assessment.

Exhibit of Peer Review Process

One of the goals for all FYC courses states that students will "demonstrate an ability to critique the writing of themselves and others." For this exhibit, which speaks directly to that goal, you will select and post to your portfolio one of the peer reviews that you have written during the semester, including commentary to help the reader understand your peer review process. One option is to choose a review you completed for one of your classmate's papers. Try to choose one that you believe was helpful and focused; you might want to ask your classmates about which ones were helpful to them. You may also copy and paste together several brief examples of peer reviews you have completed and construct a new document with inserted commentary. Explanations about the assigned peer review are often helpful here, too. As in the previous case, the Peer Review Exhibit gives you a chance to demonstrate not so much your best products for the semester, as the skill set that you have built up over the course. As with the Composing/Peer Review Exhibit, the Peer Review Exhibit gives you a chance to reflect on your progress throughout the semester and to perform a self-assessment.

Wild Card

This exhibit is up to you. The only limitations are that your Wild Card 1) must be an electronic file or link that "fits" in your <emma>™ portfolio; and 2) must include some of your writing, which may appear as captions, short descriptions, or introductory commentary. In the past, students have submitted journals, papers, photos with captions, short stories, poems, letters, song lyrics, scans of drawings with comments, news articles, podcasts, and music files. Some students create new exhibits especially to fit with their portfolio theme. In thinking about selecting or creating a Wild Card, consider how it fits into your overall portfolio rationale and how its inclusion will impact ethos and pathos.

Special Note on Presentation and Publication of your ePortfolio

Importance: The electronic portfolio, as the capstone project that showcases your achievements and learning, is very important; it counts for about 30% of your final grade.

Digital Publication: The ePortfolio is not merely a loose collection of word-processed documents, but a **unified digital artifact** whose parts fit together in a rational and harmonious manner. It is therefore not enough to just put your final documents in the Portfolio Prep folder. You must construct the ePortfolio using the Portfolio Tool; this is the only way that your readers can access your work. If you do not complete the ePortfolio properly, you may receive a grade of zero for this important project.

Presentation and Design: Just as the Grading Rubric considers Presentation and Document Design as important to the rhetorical success of your essays, so too does the ePortfolio. Your portfolio therefore must meet the highest standards for presentation and document design; failure to do so will seriously hurt your grade for the ePortfolio.

Readability and Access: Finally, this is an electronic (rather than a print) portfolio that will be read online by two different readers. It is your responsibility to make sure that:

- the front page of your ePort (biography and image) and all of the exhibits display properly without significant formatting issues;
- all exhibits are in one of the acceptable file formats (see below);
- can be navigated easily and efficiently by your readers.

Open your portfolio on several different computers and click through all the exhibits to make sure that the portfolio is reader-friendly.

How Are FYC Portfolios Evaluated?

At the end of the semester, every FYC student's <emma>™ Portfolio is read by at least two FYC teachers: his or her own teacher and one other. The presence of a second reader gives writers another real reader for their work. If the scores assigned to any portfolio differ by ten or more points, a third FYC teacher also reads and scores that Portfolio. To arrive at a final portfolio score, the two closest scores awarded are averaged. The Portfolio grade counts towards approximately 1/3 of an FYC student's final course grade. (See your teacher's syllabus for more information.)

In order to evaluate them, teachers read portfolios holistically. This means that the readers "norm" themselves, getting a sense of what "constitutes" an A, B, C, etc. among the group of portfolios that they are reading, then judge each portfolio as a whole, assigning it a single grade. As teachers read through students' portfolios, they particularly gauge how well a student's Introductory Reflective Essay (IRE) describes the content found in the other exhibits and whether or not the student has been able to use writing to express his or her own encounter with goals and evaluative criteria of the course. In other words, expect FYC teachers to use the IRE as a guide for reading your other documents, in order to get a sense of how well they match the expectations you set up in your Introduction. Of course, teachers always look for evidence of care, originality, hard work, and excellent writing, but in the portfolio we are also interested in students' ability to write reflectively and accurately about their own writing.

In addition, teachers often use the Rubric below, based on the standard FYC rubric and using the same or similar terminology, to help them get started when they are beginning to evaluate portfolios each semester. They may also point you towards this rubric to help you evaluate your own or your classmates' portfolio during a work-shop.

Technical Note: Acceptable File Formats for ePortfolio Exhibits

Because at least two teachers must be able to read successfully your ePortfolio online and not all teachers will have available the proprietary word processing package contained on your personal computer, the FYC Program accepts only the following file formats for ePortfolio Exhibits that are primarily text documents:

- OpenOffice ODT
- PDF
- <emma> eDocuments

Open Office documents: While some teachers allow students to produce their work in Microsoft Word during the semester, there can be significant formatting issues when translating Microsoft Word (.doc and .docx) documents into OpenOffice documents; we strongly recommend that for you use OpenOffice, which is freely available for download from the Web, throughout the semester as your chosen FYC word processor.

<emma> eDocuments: This accepted format is easy to use; eDocs have the added advantage of allowing you to do all your writing and editing in the web browser itself. If you use eDocs for the biography, however, you will have limited options for display. Most writers prefer OpenOffice for the portfolio's Biography.

PDF documents: Students who include a large number of images in their documents or have special design and formatting needs often choose to upload the documents in their portfolios as PDF documents. This is the only format in which you can be absolutely sure that the document appears exactly the same in your word processor and the web display.

ELECTRONIC PORTFOLIO RUBRIC

BIOGRAPHY AND IMAGE
- Is present and complete;
- Is carefully proofread and edited, with very few errors of a grammatical, mechanical, or typographic nature.
  [CCC]_____

- Shows clear and appropriate awareness of audience;
- Gives a coherent picture of the writer.
  [SP]_____

- Is distinctive for its:
  - imaginative quality;
  - extraordinary and effective care in craftsmanship and presentation;
  - prose style;
  - compelling authorial voice;
  - persuasive argumentation.
  [DIST]_____

INTRODUCTORY REFLECTIVE ESSAY
- Is present and complete;
- Makes a clear and complete statement about the writer's ethos, development, and/or skill set that is more than an autobiographical narrative or list of exhibits (unity-thesis);
- Offers a clear rationale for the choice of exhibits and their order (unity-organization);
- Explains the role of each exhibit in the overall portfolio and in proving the thesis (evidence);
- Is carefully proofread and edited, with very few errors of a grammatical, mechanical, or typographic nature.
  [CCC]_____

- Offers a strong, and vivid understanding of the writer and writing (audience awareness);
- Is particularly persuasive about how exhibits contribute to the whole portfolio (coherence).
- Is carefully written and edited, with essentially no errors of a grammatical, mechanical, or typographic nature.
  [SP]_____

- Is distinctive for its:
  - imaginative quality;
  - extraordinary and effective care in craftsmanship and presentation;

- prose style;
- compelling authorial voice;
- persuasive argumentation.

[DIST]_____

TWO REVISED CLASS ESSAYS

- Are present and complete;
- At a minimum, meet the FYC Rubric qualifications for CCC;
- Are carefully proofread and edited, with very few errors of a grammatical, mechanical, or typographic nature.

[CCC]_____

- At a minimum, meet the FYC Rubric qualifications for SP.

[SP]_____

- At a minimum, meet the FYC Rubric qualifications for a DIST or a "high" SP that shows extraordinary thoughtfulness and care.

[DIST]_____

EXHIBIT OF COMPOSING AND/OR REVISION PROCESS

- Is present and complete;
- Offers a clear and complete statement about and/or example of the composing and/or revision process (unity);
- Supports that thesis with specific examples (evidence);
- Presents the examples in a logical manner (unity-organization);
- Is carefully written, edited, and proofread, with essentially no distracting errors of a grammatical, mechanical, or typographic nature.

[CCC]_____

- Offers strong and vivid examples of the writer and writing (audience awareness);
- Is particularly persuasive about how the examples support the thesis (coherence).

[SP]_____

- Is distinctive for its:
    - imaginative quality;
    - extraordinary and effective care in craftsmanship and presentation;
    - prose style;
    - compelling authorial voice;
    - persuasive argumentation.

[DIST]_____

EXHIBIT OF PEER REVIEW PROCESS
- Is present and complete;
- Offers a clear exhibit of a peer review (unity);
- Arranges one or more examples of peer review in a logical manner (unity-organization);
- Is carefully presented so that both the original and comments are easily seen. Errors in grammar or spelling don't interfere with conveying comments (presentation & design).
  [CCC]_____

- Shows a strong, and vivid understanding of the writer and commentary (audience awareness);
- Is persuasive because comments show a clear understanding and response to the work (coherence).
  [SP]_____

- Is distinctive for its:
  - imaginative quality;
  - extraordinary and effective care in craftsmanship and presentation;
  - prose style;
  - compelling authorial voice;
  - persuasive argumentation.
  [DIST]_____

WILD CARD
- Is present and complete;
- Fits into the portfolio as a whole in a logical way that is described in the introductory reflective essay;
- Is carefully written, edited, and proofread, with few errors of a grammatical, mechanical, or typographic nature that distract from the purpose of the exhibit.
  [CCC]_____

- Offers a strong, and vivid understanding of the writer and writing (audience awareness).
  [SP]_____

- Is distinctive for its:
  - imaginative quality;
  - extraordinary and effective care in craftsmanship and presentation;
  - prose style;
  - compelling authorial voice;
  - persuasive argumentation.
  [DIST]_____

CHAPTER SEVEN

Academic Honesty and Plagiarism

7

UGA Academic Honesty Policy

The University of Georgia is committed to "A Culture of Honesty." The First-year Composition Program supports this commitment and follows strictly the university's policies and procedures for dealing with possible instances of academic dishonesty. Information about "A Culture of Honesty" and the "UGA Academic Honesty Policy" and procedures can be found at the web site of the Office of the Vice President for Instruction: http://www.uga.edu/honesty/.

All FYC students should become very familiar with this site!

Plagiarism

A particular form of academic dishonesty that First-year Composition students need to understand and guard against is plagiarism. *Plagiarism* is the use of another's words or interpretations without giving credit. Plagiarism occurs when writers fail to use quotation marks to indicate exact words from a source, when they fail to paraphrase a passage completely, or when they fail to cite the source of any quotation or paraphrase.

In recent years, cutting and pasting information from the World Wide Web can lead students to commit plagiarism, particularly when they forget where the information was copied from or lose the ability to tell the difference between their own words and those copied from an electronic source. Students should also take particular care to ensure that the Wild Card exhibit for the final electronic portfolio is their own work and identifies correctly any work by other authors included in that piece.

To avoid plagiarism, writers should always:

1. Put quotation marks around any words from sources. When writers use an open book for writing a paper or in taking notes, or when writers take notes by cutting and pasting from an online source or website, they must be careful not to plagiarize unintentionally.

2. Paraphrase material completely; changing or rearranging a few words or the tense of a verb is not paraphrasing. Writers should read the passage to be used,

close the source book or minimize the web browser, and then write in their own words what they have read. They should then compare the paraphrase to the source; if by chance key words from the original are included, these should be changed or enclosed in quotation marks.

3. Give accurate and complete citations for all material. *The St. Martin's Handbook* gives extensive information about MLA documentation style. Writers should refer to this source when writing a paper or should consult with their instructor as to what form is required in a particular course.

4. Avoid borrowing entire arguments or approaches to a subject from another writer. In general, college papers should argue an original idea and should not be paraphrases of another writer's work. All papers that students submit must be their original work. The advantages to writers of a well-documented paper are obvious: documentation shows that writers know their subjects, and the citations give their ideas validity.

Workshop
How Not to Plagiarize

The Provost of the University of Georgia has asked FYC to conduct a program-wide workshop on plagiarism in every ENGL 1101, 1102, and 1102M class in order to support the University of Georgia's efforts to educate students on this subject. The Workshop seeks to inform students about the nature of plagiarism and about ways to avoid plagiarism in their writing. It is designed in two parts, to be completed over two-three different class periods, but instructors may wish to complete the entire workshop within one class period. Your teacher will give you specific instructions.

Part 1: Recognizing Plagiarism

Before your in-class Plagiarism Workshop:

1. Read this handout, "**How Not to Plagiarize**," for the Plagiarism Workshop.

2. Review the discussion of "**Academic Honesty and Plagiarism**" in the *First-year Composition Guide, University of Georgia* (Fountainhead Press).

3. On the Web, follow the link to the University of Georgia site on Academic Honesty that is referenced in this section of *First-year Composition Guide.* Review carefully the policies and procedures outlined there.

4. Review **Chapter 14** of *The St. Martin's Handbook*, 7th edition on "**Acknowledging Sources and Avoiding Plagiarism.**"

5. On the Web, go to **"The St. Martin's Tutorial on Plagiarism."** (See the URL for the website in Works Cited, below). When you log on as a student for the first

time, you will be asked for certain information, including the email address of your instructor so that she or he can receive email reports of your quiz and exercise results. If your instructor wishes for you to provide his or her email and receive your results, she or he will tell you at this time.

6. Read through the entire online tutorial. Read with special care the section on **"Knowing Which Sources to Acknowledge."**

7. At home / before class, work through the **"Exercise: Acknowledging Sources."** Be prepared to discuss the results of this exercise and the differences between "common knowledge" and sources that must be acknowledged at your next class meeting.

8. In-class: Discuss Homework results.

Part 2: Acknowledging Sources

Before your in-class Plagiarism Workshop:

1. Review carefully the sections on **"Taking Notes"** and **"Documenting Sources"** in "**The St. Martin's Tutorial on Avoiding Plagiarism**."

2. Work through and submit the exercises on **"Recognizing Summaries," "Recognizing Paraphrases," and "Recognizing Integrated Quotations."** In your next class meeting, be prepared to discuss the results and implications of these exercises. Be prepared to ask whatever questions you may have about how to avoid plagiarism in summaries and paraphrases and about integrating quotations.

The goals of this Workshop are to support the UGA Academic Honesty Pledge—"I will be academically honest in all of my academic work and will not tolerate academic dishonesty of others"—and to help students use sources wisely in their essays.

Part 3: Follow-up Exercise

1. In-class: Work through and discuss the Handout in this book entitled "Citation or Plagiarism? On Using Sources Wisely."

Resources

Academic Honesty (A Culture of Honesty). Office of the Vice President for Instruction. http://www.uga.edu/honesty/.

FYC at UGA Website. http://web.english.uga.edu/newsite/fyc/home.html.

Price, Margaret. "The St. Martin's Tutorial on Avoiding Plagiarism." http://bcs.bedfordstmartins.com/plagiarismtutorial/.

"MLA Handbook Bibliographic Format for References." Research Central. http://www.libs.uga.edu/ref/mlastyle.html.

The St. Martin's Handbook Website. http://bcs.bedfordstmartins.com/smhandbook/default.asp.

Citation or Plagiarism? On Using Sources Wisely

First-year Composition, University of Georgia

Scenario #1 (completely fictional, with apologies to bears): Student A is writing an essay arguing that because bears have become a public nuisance in Missoula, Montana, a law should be passed allowing law enforcement officers to trap and release the most difficult genre of bear, the Asiatic black bear. She has found a description of this bear on the website listed below:

> **Description:** *The Asiatic black bear is a medium sized bear with a body length of 50 to 74 inches and weighing between 220 and 440 pounds. Females are smaller than males. They are normally blackish in color, with lighter muzzles and a distinct V-shaped patch of cream colored fur on their chest. A brown phase also occurs. The ears of an Asiatic black bear appear much larger than those of other bear species.*
>
> *http://www.bearden.org/asibear.html*

One body paragraph of Student A's paper reads as follows:

> This proposed law, which would allow police officers to take action against marauding bears, would be particularly helpful in stopping the rampages of the Asiatic black bears of Missoula, an easily recognizable pest on the streets of this city. The Asiatic black bear is a medium sized bear with a body length of 50 to 74 inches and weighing between 220 and 440 pounds. Females are smaller than males. They are normally blackish in color, with lighter muzzles and a distinct V-shaped patch of cream colored fur on their chest. A brown phase also occurs. The ears of an Asiatic black bear appear much larger than those of other bear species ("Asiatic Black Bear"). If the black bear were stopped, the city could get back to normal. We should take action now!

Citation or plagiarism? You make the call.

Scenario #2 (completely fictional, with apologies to bears): Student B is writing in defense of the Asian black bear, which is an endangered species in some countries.

He has found the same website, which he uses as well in his paper. One body paragraph of Student B's reads as follow:

> Allowing officers to target the Asian black bear in their efforts to clean up the streets of Missoula is completely misguided because any person should be able to recognize and avoid the black bear, whose appearance is quite distinctive. The Asiatic black bear is a medium sized bear with a body length of 50 to 74 inches and weighing between 220 and 440 pounds. Females, who are smaller than males, are black and have lighter muzzles and a patch of yellow fur on their chest. Furthermore, the Asiatic black bear has larger ears than other bears ("Asiatic Black Bear").

Citation or plagiarism? You make the call.

CHAPTER EIGHT

Resources

8

Students who are new to the University of Georgia are often unsure about what services are available to them and where to go for help of various kinds. This section offers you places to go for help with writing, research, and personal issues.

Tutoring and Help with Writing

The university offers writers in First-year Composition a wide range of services at different locations across campus:

The UGA Writing Center

The Department of English operates the UGA Writing Center in Park Hall 66, and First-year Composition students are welcome to use its services during their FYC classes and anytime during their careers at the University of Georgia. Serving students across the campus, the Writing Center has special tutoring services for ESOL students. The Writing Center also operates a satellite center in the Science Library (South Campus Writing Center) and holds drop-in sessions at the Miller Learning Center (MLC). For locations of these satellite centers and hours at all three locations, see the Writing Center's website at: http://writingcenter.english.uga.edu/.

Students can also get further information about services offered by the Writing Center and sign up for an appointment through the Online Appointment Signup System, which is available on the website. The Writing Center also accepts drop-in clients.

Milledge Hall Tutoring Center

Located in Milledge Hall, the Division of Academic Enhancement provides appointment-based, drop-in, and online tutoring for undergraduate and graduate students across campus and disciplines. Experienced English as a Second Language specialists are available to work in person with multi-lingual students. In addition to Milledge Hall, Academic Enhancement tutoring services are available in the Miller Learning Center, in the South Campus Writing Center, located in the Science Library. For more information, go to: http://www.uga.edu/dae/ and look under Services, Tutoring.

Research

One of the biggest changes that students notice about the change between high school and university is the fact that here they are expected to do research on their own and that they are expected to know how to do quality research in a range of academic disciplines. These are big expectations, but fortunately, the UGA Libraries can help.

The UGA Libraries

Homepage: http://www.libs.uga.edu

UGA has the largest library in the state, with 4.6 million books, thousands of periodical subscriptions, hundreds of online databases, and many librarians to help you navigate through it all. Libraries on campus include:

- Main Library on North Campus: humanities, social sciences, and business;
- Science Library on South Campus: science, technology, and agriculture;
- Miller Learning Center: electronic library resources.

For college-level research projects and papers, your instructors will expect you to use *published scholarly* resources and *critically evaluate* any sources you take from the web. Fear not: in addition to its large book collection, the Libraries subscribe to many online databases that include articles and books suitable for college research. Starting at the Libraries' homepage, follow the *Books & More* tab to GIL-Find, the online catalog of books in the UGA Libraries' collections. To find articles from magazines, scholarly journals, and newspapers, start with the default *Multi-Search* tab. Multi-Search lets you limit your results to only full-text articles, only scholarly articles, only newspapers, only ebooks, and other options.

More resources are under the *Articles & Databases* tab:

- *For English 1101*, use **Academic Search Complete** for magazine and scholarly journal articles, **LexisNexis Academic** for newspaper articles and TV/radio transcripts, and **CQ Researcher Plus** for analyses of current issues;
- *For English 1102/1102M*, use **JSTOR** or the **MLA International Bibliography** for literary criticism published in scholarly journals, and **Literature Resource Center** for biographies of authors.

Ask a librarian for help choosing keywords, creating a search strategy, and for suggestions for additional discipline-specific databases and resources for your projects.

If you are searching from on campus (including the dorms), you won't need a password to use any of these online resources. To search from off campus, get the password under *GALILEO Password* on the Libraries' homepage.

Need help? Use our "Ask a Librarian" chat box on the library homepage or ask at the reference desk in any of the library buildings. The research support desk at the Main and Science libraries is located on the entry floors; the research support desk at the Miller Learning Center is located at the top of the stairs on the third floor. One-on-one research conferences with librarians are also available; sign up at http://www.libs.uga.edu/ref/instruction/conform.html.

CAPS (Counseling and Psychological Services)

Everyone can use help and support at some time during his or her academic career: "Counseling and Psychiatric Services (CAPS) is dedicated to providing the best available counseling, psychiatric and psychological testing services. CAPS provides short-term individual and couples counseling, group counseling, crisis intervention, medication evaluation and monitoring, psychological testing, and makes referrals to resources on and off-campus when appropriate" (http://www.uhs.uga.edu/caps/). For more information, call 706-542-2273 or see the website from which this text was taken: http://www.uhs.uga.edu/caps/.

Whatever assistance you need, you can find it at the University of Georgia. If you are having problems—whether personal or academic—you can also ask your teacher for a referral to the proper resource.

CHAPTER NINE

What Comes Next?

Research into the writing process shows that the use of writing as a part of the learning process and frequency of writing are both crucial to improving and even just maintaining the writing skills and critical thinking processes that students acquire in their First-year Composition classes. What is more, employers consistently report on the importance of basic communication skills, especially in writing, for the workplace. Research has also suggested a close connection between reading and writing proficiency, and UGA students have shown that they enjoy reading and discussing books outside their formal classes. For all of these reasons, the University of Georgia encourages you to seek out other opportunities for practice in reading and writing. We would like to conclude by telling you about future opportunities to practice your literacy skills and to use writing as a powerful learning tool.

Writing Certificate Program

Beginning in 2008-2009, the University of Georgia began offering a certificate program in writing. The purpose of the Writing Certificate Program is to give undergraduate students from all colleges and majors at the University of Georgia an opportunity to develop and document their writing skills as they move from First-year Composition through the core curriculum and their academic majors en route to further education, professional training, or the workplace. Their writing skills will be developed in the context of their particular academic studies and interests and will be documented with a published electronic portfolio that presents and reflects on the students' writing projects and experiences throughout their undergraduate career. The writing done for the program will enhance students' understanding and accomplishment in their chosen field of study and will provide evidence to outside evaluators (such as admissions committees or employers) of the students' critical thinking, research, and communication skills, plus their understanding of genres and conventions of writing within their chosen discipline. For more information about the program and its benefits, visit: http://www.ctl.uga.edu/writing_certificate/.

Writing Intensive Program (WIP)

The Writing Intensive Program at the University of Georgia offers students multiple opportunities to strengthen their writing throughout their undergraduate experience by offering writing-intensive courses throughout the university in varying disciplines—from Art History to Biology to Music to Sociology, for example. A key goal of the program is to foster student writing *in the disciplines*, by helping students understand the conventions—or "ways of knowing"—of a particular discipline: how knowledge is constructed and communicated, and what rules of evidence and argumentation are practiced. To accomplish the goals of the program, each Writing Intensive Program (WIP) course is supported by a specially trained "writing coach," who works with students to improve their writing and performance in the course by providing constructive and personal feedback. The advantages of this coaching—and WIP courses, in general—are many. A compelling majority of students enrolled in these courses consistently report that their experience with the Writing Intensive Program strengthened their writing skills; built their confidence in the writing process; encouraged a deeper engagement in course reading, discussions, and assignments; taught them the writing conventions of their discipline; heightened their critical thinking skills; and prepared them for writing in other courses and future goals, such as graduate school or career-related work. **All WIP courses count toward requirements for the Writing Certificate Program**.

For more information about the program and its benefits, as well as for a list of current WIP courses, visit: http:// www.wip.uga.edu.

The Major and Minor in English

The skills in writing and critical thinking that you have learned in First-year Composition will serve you well if you decide to major or minor in English. English majors learn to read, interpret, and analyze texts (novels, stories, plays, films, poems, essays, images, and other forms of cultural production) and to write with poise, brevity, and elegance. Majors can choose Areas of Emphasis for their Program of Study; areas of emphasis include Creative Writing, Multicultural American Literature, Rhetoric and Composition, Humanities Computing, Medieval Literature, Studies in the Novel, Advanced Studies in English, Interdisciplinary Renaissance Studies, and English Language Studies. Majors and minors can go on to careers in almost anything: teaching, publishing, law, journalism, management, human resources, medicine, grant-writing, screen-writing, technical writing, and so on. You can find more information about the English major and minor at the program website: http://www.english.uga.edu/news-ite/undergrad/home.html.

Declared English majors may join our job club, "19 Weeks," and take ENGL 4001, Careers for English Majors. We also encourage potential majors to take ENGL 4000, Introduction to the English Major.

Bulldog Book Club

If you want to read for pleasure, check out the Bulldog Book Club! Each meeting is a blue card event; UGA students choose the books. For more information, check the UGA Libraries News & Events blog at: http://www.libs.uga.edu/blog/.

Advanced Courses in Writing

The English Department offers several upper-division courses in writing that are open to students in other majors. The Academic Enhancement Program, housed in Milledge Hall, also offers an array of writing classes for native and non-native speakers.

UNIV 1105. Improving Grammar, Usage, and Style.
3 hours.
Oasis Title: IMPROVING GRAMMAR.

> This course teaches students to master formal grammar rules and terminology, to achieve a clear, fluent writing style, and to recognize common problems of usage so that they can effectively write and edit papers for academic and professional audiences.
>
> **Note**: Students may enroll in this course simultaneously with ENGL 1101.

UNIV 1117. Basic Composition for Multilingual Writers.
3 hours (institutional credit).
Oasis Title: MULTILINGUAL COMP.

> This course is designed for both undergraduate and graduate students whose first language is not English. Its objectives include mastering English grammar, idioms, and sentence structure; building an academic vocabulary; and composing short academic papers. The course emphasizes problems that non-native speakers typically experience with proofreading, revision, and writing for an American audience. Assignments may be tailored to students' majors.
>
> **Note**: This course carries institutional credit and will not count toward graduation.

ENGL 3590. Technical Communication.
3 hours.
Oasis Title: TECH AND PROF COMM.

> This course deals with writing in the professional domains, with an emphasis on research methods, clear and accurate presentation of ideas and data, and computer-mediated communication. If you want an introduction to the role of writing in the workplace, this course would be for you.

ENGL 3600. Advanced Composition.
3 hours.
Oasis Title: ADV COMPOSITION.

> Advanced Composition focuses less on professional contexts than on writing as a process, with an emphasis on the conventions of discourse situations, inven-

tion, revision, editorial skills, and document design. This course is particularly useful for students who want to practice and improve their academic writing.

ENGL 4832. Writing for the World Wide Web.

3 hours.
Oasis Title: WRITING FOR THE WEB.

This class deals with both the theory and practice of writing for the World Wide Web. Here you will learn to use the basic tools to construct web sites and be introduced to other advanced technologies useful for academic and professional writers.

ENGL 4833. Composition Theory and Pedagogy.

3 hours.
Oasis Title: COMP PEDAGOGY

This course introduces you to the history and theories of college composition teaching. With a strong practical emphasis, ENGL 4833 prepares students to work as college writing tutors or as classroom writing assistants.

Donald E. Barnett Awards for 2010-2011

10

Donald E. Barnett Awards for 2010-2011

Each year, the First-year Composition Program recognizes excellent writing in English 1101, 1102, and 1102M by presenting three Barnett Awards. Named in honor of Donald E. Barnett, who directed the Freshman English Program for many years, the awards consist of cash prizes and publication of the winning essays in the *First-year Composition Guide* required of all students registered in our courses and on the FYC site at: http://www.english.uga.edu/newsite/fyc/barnett.html.

Thomas Parrott served in the U.S. Air Force for over six years before attending UGA; he wrote this essay for an English 1101E special topics class on Social Networking, the Entertainment Industry, and Consumers. Thomas's English 1101 Barnett essay follows one of the oldest prose forms—the true "essay," from the Old French essai, *meaning "a trial, testing, proof, experiment" (Oxford English Dictionary). Traditionally, the essay is thought to follow the writer's train of thought and to have no other organizational principle—or a thesis, for that matter. But the essay's conversational tone and look of spontaneity are deceptive. Although it may be implicit rather than boldly stated, Thomas's essay has a definite thesis; it also makes an argument—if you'll try, you will see that you can easily restate that argument in more formal terms. The essay is "FYC distinctive" because it is insightful, unique, and funny, according to his instructor.*

ENGL1101E

Student: Thomas Parrott

Teacher: Allison Lenhardt

Diary of a Facebook Convert

One of my foremost traits is the simple reality that I am not a social person. Others are anxious to go downtown on the weekend, while I'm perfectly happy sitting at home and reading a book. I avoid being the center of attention and prefer the freedom of being relatively unnoticed in the crowd, enabling me to do my own thing. It may come as something of a shock, then, when I reveal that I am a habitual Facebook user, one of those people who logs in on their phone just to find out if anything new has been posted in the last fifteen minutes. I didn't become an internet socialite overnight; rather, it was the result of how my opinions evolved over a significant period of time.

As I said, I didn't begin as a fan of social media. Around eight years ago, I kept a LiveJournal more as a joke than anything else and updated it only sporadically with bursts of teenage angst. I found a handful of blogs that I considered interesting enough to keep up with, but the huge numbers of random people blogging only left me confused and questioning, "Who were they trying to reach? What were they getting out of it?" Then along came MySpace, and the only real response I could muster was scorn. Somewhere in the combination of garish colors, irritating repeating music, and incomprehensible comments, the creators of the website and pages alike had managed to find a recipe to drive me away completely. I would likely have written off the whole concept if I hadn't shipped out and left Georgia behind for several years to come.

There is a phenomenon in the Air Force that I'm sure is duplicated in the other branches as well, called a "tech school marriage." In essence, people complete basic and move on to the next step in their training, only to immediately "fall in love" with a fellow trainee and be married within a month. I'm no trained psychologist, so I can't say with any assurance what causes this phenomenon, but I have my own theory: extreme homesickness you can't even admit you're feeling. People are ripped away from friends, family, and comforting surroundings and generally run ragged. They want something to hold on to and reach out to grasp anything that will make this "home." Some people choose a hasty, ill-conceived marriage. In the end, I turned to the internet to hold onto old connections.

The first time I got an opportunity to use a computer after basic training was in a dingy, old computer lab located in our dormitory building at Presidio of Monterey, the kind of place with age stains on the ceilings and gouges in the walls. The computer itself was old enough that I was worried I might have wandered into a museum, and I found myself desperately hoping that the internet had existed when the computer was built. Yet soon enough I was logged in and exchanging emails with people back home, setting up my first stretch of leave to be spent with friends and family over the Christmas exodus, when the entire base would be a ghost town as all the trainees went home. Just as easily as that, the connection between "internet" and "home" was fixed in my mind.

From there, my acceptance of social media started with online bulletin boards and a more concerted effort to get into my friends' LiveJournals. Soon enough, however, someone came to me talking about a new site that had appeared on the stage: Facebook. As was my nature at the time, I scoffed at this; even the name seemed terrible, some sort of a reference to a high school yearbook. Yet over time, more and more people I knew joined and talked about it. First, friends who were close to my age, then my sisters, and by the time I was twenty-one, even my mother and aunts were making profiles. Now, I might not like to think of myself as a man who caves to peer pressure, but when even your technophobic mother is encouraging you to "get on Facebook," eventually you have to crack.

Thus, I found myself in possession of a brand new Facebook profile. I had told myself I'd never post pictures of myself to the internet: that went out the window the same day. There were no garish color schemes, no ear-grating midis playing on endless repeat. In fact, the format was all surprisingly uniform and straightforward, easy to read. Then came the ultimate shocker: it turns out that people who you like and think are funny and entertaining in person are likely to be so even when posting a brief thought as a status. So in the end, it wasn't the application itself that won me over, approval of the format or no. Instead, in a way that was obvious in retrospect, it was the people I cared about that got me hooked in.

Hooked or not, however, I did not anticipate when Facebook would have its largest impact on me. A major part of military life is the reality of deployment. Your training instructors tell you first, "Everyone goes eventually." This mantra is repeated by supervisors and commanders, until eventually it is, indeed, your turn to go. You wake up bright and early some morning and report to a building where you and dozens to hundreds of others sit around, tired and bored and nervous, all at once. You get on the plane, sit uncomfortably for a whole day of travel, and finally, you're there, on the other side of the world from everything you know and love. Eventually, you are given a chance to use the media tent, and for me and others like me, Facebook is one of the things waiting for you. It might not be as good as being there, but you can still get a sense surprisingly quickly for how things are going back home. You can peruse a dozen statuses, laugh over pictures, and let everyone know that you're doing okay. If you're lucky, for just a moment you can even forget where you are.

Of course, these days I've left the military behind and moved on into a new stage of my life. The hair cut, the clothes, and the attitude all changed as I came to the University of Georgia, and the way I used social media changed, too. Part of it is role reversal, as I'm the one sending friends overseas the messages encouraging them to keep their chin up. My usage goes further than that, though: it's not about just keeping in touch with old friends anymore. Now it's about networking with new ones, making and maintaining the connections that are going to carry me through the college years and on into the rest of my life. As my life changes, my use of Facebook just changes too, leaving me convinced it's not going anywhere any time soon.

Now that we've charted my course from an absolute social media skeptic to a Facebook true believer, I won't claim that I don't still see flaws in the progress of social media, or that I've bought into the whole scheme. I've seen it exacerbate too much drama and provoke too many arguments all by itself, not to mention the occasional violations of privacy and the like. In the end, though, it lets me keep in touch with friends and family scattered all across the country and even the world, and if nothing else, I'm grateful for that opportunity. Just don't get me started on Twitter, as I still can't quite take that sort of nonsense. At least, until my mother gets an account.

Kaitlyn Downs's English 1102 Barnett essay is a traditional literary analysis that explores a particular theme throughout a literary work, in this case William Shakespeare's The Taming of the Shrew. *She supports her argument with evidence from the primary text (in this case, summary, paraphrase, and quotation) and from secondary sources (in this case, literary criticism). What make Kaitlyn's essay particularly striking are: the way in which the author leads the reader carefully through the stages of her argument, almost as though they were discussing the issue together; the complexity of the essay's thesis, which concludes not only that appearance and reality are indistinguishable, but also the larger truth that believing in false appearances can create real changes in a person; and, as her instructor puts it, the surprising way Kaitlyn's essay "hones in on a character that is usually overlooked."*

ENGL1102
Student: Kaitlyn Downs
Teacher: Beth Kozinsky

Character Identity in *The Taming of the Shrew*

If something walks like a duck, quacks like a duck, and acts like a duck, is it a duck? Probably, but what if this "duck" is really just a confused chicken? At this point, the question of identity comes into play. Is the chicken then considered a duck because its actions all point towards that of the distinctive aquatic bird? Or does the chicken's actual reality as a chicken, its feathery DNA, matter more in this discussion? Identity in *The Taming of the Shrew* acts the same way. Highlighting the nature of identity, Shakespeare uses the story of Christopher Sly's taming and its counterpart, Kate's taming, to show that appearance becomes reality. Ultimately, the characters in *The Taming of the Shrew* blur the lines between reality and illusion, making them one and the same.

In the beginning of the play, the small part of dialogue concerning Christopher Sly shows the phenomenon of illusion becoming reality. A rich lord abducts Sly, a drunken beggar, and plays a trick on him: "What think you, if he were . . . wrapped in sweet clothes, rings put upon his fingers, a most delicious banquet by his bed . . . Would not the beggar then forget himself?" (Shakespeare, *Taming of the Shrew*, Ind. 1.33-37). When Sly awakens in an unfamiliar setting, he questions the truth of his predicament, but eventually, he wholeheartedly accepts the illusion that "[he is] a lord indeed, and not a tinker nor Christopher Sly" (Ind. 2.68-69). Because Sly sees that he possesses all the characteristics of a lord — fine clothes, dedicated servants, a noble "wife" — he immediately accepts the façade.

When he accepts his pseudo-nobility, Sly's paradigm of his own reality shifts completely. He notices that he possesses all the characteristics of a lord and adjusts his own identity accordingly: he becomes the lord. Initially, the changes in Sly are merely superficial; he gains obedient servants, nice clothes, and delicious food. Nothing about his personality should change, but it does. Not only does Sly state his belief in his nobility, but he also exhibits changes in his language, demonstrating the sincerity of his personality change. Critic Joseph Tate cites the fact that Sly's form of speaking changes from prose, indicating a peasant, to blank verse, traditionally a form of speech used by poets and playwrights for aristocratic speech (106). Christopher Sly's "[rise] to verse and into nobility" indicates that a real change occurs in Sly's perception of himself and, therefore, in his actual identity (106).

Still the question remains: is Sly a true lord or just an overdressed, indulged peasant tricked by a cruel, bored aristocrat? Shakespeare's treatment of Sly's story makes it seem as though he remains a lord. Introduced to Sly at the start, the audience naturally waits for his storyline to be continued, but Shakespeare never finishes it. Sly appears for the final time at the end of the first scene of act 1, and in this appearance, he merely complements the play itself (1.1.243-44). This unfinished plot device serves as a purposeful reminder that illusion has become reality — that Sly's illusory nobility becomes actual nobility. Supporting this claim, Tate points out that while the play's plot implies that characters assume and shed disguises easily, "the induction's incompleteness proposes the opposite"(Tate 107). Sly never "return[s] to a world of stable identities" and stays eternally as a lord (107). The implication that Christopher Sly becomes a lord and stays one indelibly within the play supports the idea that his identity changes permanently on the basis of appearance; the chicken has evolved into a duck.

Immediately after Sly's final line, Petruchio bursts on stage, establishing his identity as a bossy, violent, and outgoing young man. Although Petruchio never disguises his personality or intentions, his act of taming Kate contributes an additional example of how illusion and appearance become the reality of a situation. Petruchio, in an effort to tame Kate, devises a scheme in which he describes her behavior contradictory to what she actually does. For instance, "Say that she rail, why then [he would tell] her plain she sings as sweetly as a nightingale. Say that she frown, [he would say] she looks as clear as morning roses" (2.1.166-69). His ruse transforms Kate's identity from the shrewish spinster seen at the beginning into the dutiful wife whose speech at the end of the play indicates her "new-built virtue and obedience" (5.2.122). She is even respectful to her husband, to the point of calling him "sir" (5.2.105). Cecil C. Seronsy proposes that "Petruchio's method [of taming] is to suppose or assume qualities in [Kate] that no one else . . . suspects. What he assumes as apparently false turns out to be startlingly true" (19). Therefore, Kate eventually becomes what Petruchio presents her as. Although at first Petruchio's descriptions of Kate seem only like his way to "kill [her] with kindness" (4.1.181), "his 'treatment' [steadily unfolds to show] her really fine qualities: patience, practical good sense, a capacity for humor, and finally obedience, all of which she comes gradually to manifest in a spirit" (Seronsy 19). In the end, Kate turns into the "modest . . . dove" Petruchio claims her to be, demonstrating again that illusion has become reality (2.1.289).

Kate, the shrew and eponymous character of the play, raises the most questions about the reality of appearance. The most obvious question about Kate is whether she is truly tamed at the very end of the play. A less common, but equally interesting question is whether Kate is, in reality, a shrew. Are her bad attitude and violent tendencies only armor that Kate dons to protect herself from vulnerability and rejection? Perhaps. Several instances in the play imply that Kate is, in fact, gentler than she initially appears: the fact that Kate cries when Petruchio is late to the wedding; her allowance of her marriage to Petruchio in the first place; and her sometimes reasonable pleas to Petruchio at the beginning of their marriage. These subtle details, however, become lost within the prominent examples of Kate's fiery temper: yelling at her suitor; tying up her sister Bianca; and smashing an instrument over her tutor's head, to name a few. Does it matter if her shrewish nature is merely armor? If everyone that has ever met Kate agrees that she is a shrew, even calling her "Katherine the curst," then it does not really make a difference if it is a charade (1.2.121). Therefore, Kate's relatives and neighbors define her identity, instead of Kate defining herself by how she feels. By "believing that Katherine is a shrew [her community] makes her one, because that is the only subject position [they allow] her" (Crocker 145). Because of the unpleasant outward appearance she gives off, Kate's armor becomes a reality, regardless of what she feels inside.

The last question of appearance versus reality is probably the most critical and common question of the play: is Kate really tamed? Well, she appears to be. At the end of the play in act 5, she obeys Petruchio, responding to his summons, unlike the other two wives. Her father seems to genuinely believe that "she is changed as she had never been" (5.2.119). She even gives a seemingly scolding speech to the other two wives, preaching the belief that "thy husband is thy lord, thy life, thy keeper, / Thy head, thy sovereign" (5.2.150-51). Although no critic and certainly no undergraduate dabbler in Shakespeare can say for sure the sincerity of Kate's taming, I believe that many elements of the play combine to give a clearer perspective on this question. Christopher Sly's story, a parallel in both situation and location within the play, paves the way for Kate's reversal of personality. Sly's identity transformation not only exhibits the nature of appearance becoming reality, but also leads the way for Kate's complete reversal of identity from headstrong shrew to obedient wife in the final act of the play. By creating perfectly parallel circumstances, not only in situation, but also in location within the play, Shakespeare draws attention to the theme of illusion becoming reality, and perhaps even prepares the audience for the legitimacy of Kate's transformation.

Shakespeare manages to answer the question of the duck. If something has all the characteristics of something else, it actually becomes, in all practical ways, that something else. He says that appearance is reality, or at least, it is the only reality that matters. Because of the analysis of Shakespeare's use of Christopher Sly, Petruchio's deception in taming, and Kate's actual nature as a shrew, the dominant question of the play grows clearer: whether or not Kate truly alters her thinking and personality to become "tamed." Because of Shakespeare's treatment of the rest of the play, it becomes evident that Kate's illusion becomes the reality of her situation, and she, in all practical sense of the word, is tamed.

Works Cited

Crocker, Holly A. "Affective Resistance: Performing Passivity and Playing A-Part in *The Taming of the Shrew*." *Shakespeare Quarterly* 54.2 (2003): 142-59. Web. 6 May 2010.

Seronsy, Cecil C. "'Supposes' as the Unifying Theme in *The Taming of the Shrew*." *Shakespeare Quarterly* 14.1 (1963): 15-30. Web. 6 May 2010.

Shakespeare, William. *The Taming of the Shrew*. *Prentice Hall Literature Portfolio*. Ed. Christy Desmet *et al*. Upper Saddle River, N.J.: Prentice Hall, 2007. 772-850. Print. 6 May 2010.

Tate, Joseph. "Shakespeare, Prose and Verse: Unreadable Forms." Diss. University of Washington, 2005. Web. 6 May 2010.

Deanna Stevens's English 1102M Barnett essay is a comparison-and-contrast between two poems that approach the same cultural problem—Native Americans' alienation from city culture—in different ways. Deanna does a fine job of organizing the essay around the ideas she wants to discuss, which makes the argument flow smoothly. Impressive also is the way in which her argument analyzes the poetic form of Joy Harjo's famously experimental verse, as well as the poems' themes. Her instructor writes: "I especially love that she took her interests in art and photography and multimedia, met them in Joy Harjo's unique style, and then went a step further and really became curious about the literature itself."

ENGL 1102M

Student: Deanna Stevens

Instructor: Liz Vasconcelos-Hammock

Considering the Physical and Symbolic in Joy Harjo's "The Myth of Blackbirds" and "Hieroglyphic"

Joy Harjo is not only an author, but also a professor, playwright, filmmaker, painter, and successful musician. She is a creative force, capable of wielding any outlet of expression to articulate her experiences and memories, yet she chooses to put the ideas seen in the poems "The Myth of Blackbirds" and "Hieroglyphic" in verse. She writes about the concealed and spiritual worlds as if they were continuous with the secular world, which leaves the audience reading both a cryptic poem full of symbolism and a poem that is simultaneously natural to our understanding. In both of Harjo's poems, "The Myth of Blackbirds" and "Hieroglyphic," the consistent duality of symbolism and environment in her writing style creates a powerful appeal for the reader to experience her memories and realms of consciousness.

To grasp the transcendent significance of these works, the reader must first look at the choices Harjo makes concerning the physical structure of the poems. The first environment the reader encounters is the presentation of the verse, its aesthetic appearance, and the elements that strike us on first impression. Both works are short poems; neither exceeds more than fifty lines. The reader should also keep in mind that Harjo performs her poems in spoken verse and that she formats the written record of the poems to maintain the cadence of the work as it is originally intended to be experienced. Harjo claims to be inspired by music rather than the works of other poets and "that when she writes poetry she does not start with an image but rather a sound" (Scarry 286). The lines are non-rhyming and are not organized into typical stanzas. "The Myth of Blackbirds" and "Hieroglyphic" use free verse, a style that emphasizes the melodic quality of the spoken word without internal rhyming or a regular meter. By using free verse in all her poetry, Harjo enables the structure to emphasize word choice and natural inflections in the reading.

At the beginning of "Blackbirds," Harjo has written four quatrains, but without an obvious reason, follows these four with six more stanzas comprised of varying lengths. "Blackbirds" lacks regular meter, which creates the impression of an unorganized stream of consciousness. This choice in structure could lead the reader to look for meaning in other features of the composition. Perhaps a deeper take on this poem begins with the interpretation of the numbers she has chosen to use in the structure. Upon closer investigation, one notices that the number of lines in each stanza and the ordering of stanzas make a palindrome—5, 3, 4, 3, 5—followed by a sestet. This last stanza may be a sestet to reinforce the number six, as the last six lines of the poem are not in keeping with the first four. If noticed, the subtle use of numbers in the organization adds to the mythic value of the poetry.

The structure of "Hieroglyphic" relies mainly on the use of quatrains, with the exception of two tercets that Harjo interjects as the fifth and thirteenth of thirteen total stanzas. The poem uses free verse and organizes itself using sentences that do not correlate with the lines. Harjo writes the poem in fifty lines comprised of twenty sentences that bridge the lines in a manner that adds emphasis to the cadence of the verse. She makes heavy use of dropped lines in every stanza, using them on every even numbered line, with the exception of the tercet stanzas. The dropped lines not only make the poem visually striking, but also add emphasis to the last couple of words in each stanza. As a result, the last line of each stanza stands out dramatically and adds a sort of cryptic element to the composition of the piece. If one were to read only the dropped lines in the poem, the selected text would not align with the entire poem, but instead provide groupings of words that are striking and enigmatic, like hieroglyphs. For example, in the third stanza—"Crossing Fifth / Avenue was a trick of the imagination. It wasn't that. By / the time I had / forgiven the stolen pyramidal gateway my heart had / become a phoenix of / swallowed myths" (lines 8-12)—the words "time," "gateway," and "phoenix" are striking because the sentence structure does not fit within the stanza. In highlighting the words in the dropped lines, Harjo elicits close attention to the words she chooses to complete each quatrain and again reinforces the sound of the poem.

In "Hieroglyphic," Harjo writes of a phoenix, skeleton horses, a crocodile, and a snake as she describes her spiritual experiences in the Egyptian room and spontaneously remembers a dream from her childhood. In realizing the correlation between present moment and memory as a spiritual revelation, Harjo attempts to describe the gravity of her realization through the use of verse and symbolic writing. In creating an atmosphere that welcomes the reader into a layering of consciousness, she writes in lines 44-50:

> be born on paper. It goes something like this: when the
>   mythic spiral of time
> turned its beaded head and understood what was going
>   on, it snapped. All
>
> these years I had been sleeping in the mind of the snake,
>   June. I have to tell
> this to someone.

The snake has been seen as a symbol of rebirth, self-reflexivity, and eternal cyclic change. In "Hieroglyphic," Harjo reflects on the timeline of her life as a serpentine entity that snaps at the moment of her realization. By weaving together these dream-like images that refer to folk tales and creation myths, she references Jung's abstract archetypes, seamlessly blended within the present moment and memory. In a review of Jung's principles of symbols in religious and unconscious archetypes, Carlsson addresses this type of revelation specifically, saying, "A man [or woman] dreams about a snake, and in Jungian theory, the snake is a symbol for something the unconscious is trying to say to the individual. What the unconscious wishes to communicate depends upon the state of the individual's inner condition"

(38). Harjo introduces the concept of time as a snake in "Hieroglyphic"; she reflects upon the symbolic nature of the messages from her dream world. The reader is never more involved than in the moment of realization when Harjo puts together her memory and present experience and denies the reader any sense of linear time by combining both past and future in the present. Through myth, her most extensively used instrument, Harjo takes the reader "into the realm where anything is possible, where meaning is exploded" (Scarry 286).

In Native American tradition, animals, physical features, and elements are incorporated into folk tales as characters with human attributes. Folk tales are based on oral tradition, and "out of the earth and ancestral lands and peoples comes memory, out of memory comes the present, and the resulting interplay of tensions fuses together into story and life" (Lang 46). As in other ancient cultures such as those of the Egyptians, Greeks, and Mayans, historical symbolism follows the image of an animal and, depending on the culture, is immediately associated with a tale of spiritual significance. As seen in the fifth stanza of "The Myth of Blackbirds,"

> This is the world in which we undressed together. Within it white deer intersect with the wisdom of the hunter of grace. Horses wheel toward the morning star. Memory was always more than paper and cannot be broken by violent history or stolen by thieves of childhood. We cannot be separated in the loop of mystery between blackbirds and the memory of blackbirds. (lines 17-21)

Harjo incorporates blackbirds, white deer, and horses with the imagery of the metropolitan development of Washington, DC and draws a comparison to the natural physical features of the land of her ancestors. Blackbirds have a particularly heavy connotation throughout history in various cultures. Because of their role as scavengers and pests to farmers, they traditionally have negative and sometimes evil associations in folktales and legends. They are seen as tricksters, messengers of the gods, and omens of illness and death. Harjo describes her role as an earthly mediator between image and idea, plays with Jung's concept of archetypes, and writes, "We cannot be separated in / the loop of mystery between blackbirds and the memory of blackbirds" (line 21).

This loop of mystery cannot exist without the human as the mediator between the idea of a blackbird and the physical manifestation of this creature on earth. Carlsson defines the concept of archetypes most clearly when he states that "in the collective unconscious, that great unknown shared by all humanity, are the archetypes, the inherited forms of psychic behavior common to all men" (32). In other words, as humans, we are predisposed to think in a certain manner and associate what we perceive with names, symbols, and memories. Harjo is aware of the thin divisions between what we see, think, and feel in reality and what we remember in our unconscious states of dreaming and creative thought. Carlsson goes further to say that the rational, conscious side of our humanity is only a small portion of our awareness and that what drives us in our conscious thought is more than just the pursuit of science and knowledge, but also the desire to contact the unknown, the mysterious: the unconscious (29).

Harjo layers symbols, memories, and narratives in her poetry not only to develop the reader's interest in her experiences, but also to create an environment that could not exist without memory. In "Twin Gods Bending Over," Lang defines Harjo's poetry as "ongoing circularities of memory, story, history, and ancestral voices that work together to create and explain natural cycles underlying human existence" (46). All of these elements combine to give the audience an environment to understand Harjo's relation to the unconscious, her perception of time and her relative position in both the physical and dream realms. In "The Myth of Blackbirds," Harjo writes, "And in the predawn when we had slept for centuries in a drenching sweet / rain" (lines 22-23), giving the audience a sensuous glimpse of how she views time and location mythically. It seems that the person to whom this poem is written holds less importance than the physical and spiritual locales of which Harjo writes so tenderly. Lang continues to interpret how "landscape and story often merge into an individual voice tied simultaneously to memories of a traditional past, as well as to the life of the present" (46). In this way, the earth Harjo remembers is as much a character as the human to whom she writes.

In both "Hieroglyphic" and "The Myth of Blackbirds," Harjo creates a portal that the audience may enter through the use of symbolism and abstraction of physical and temporal space. To hear or read her poetry requires the audience to let go of preconceived notions of time-consciousness and to accept archetypal and symbolic concepts regarding myth and folklore. Harjo keeps alive the tradition of storytelling by weaving narratives within spoken word poetry and reminds us that "one has no authentic voice without memory; and without an authentic voice, one is speechless, hardly human, and unable to survive for very long" (Lang 49).

Works Cited

Carlsson, Allan. "Jung on Meaning and Symbols in Religion." *The Journal of General Education* 22.1 (1970): 29-40. *JSTOR*. Web. 24 Mar. 2011.

Harjo, Joy. "Hieroglyphic." *Ploughshares* 13.4 (1987). Web. 21 Mar. 2011.

—. "The Myth of Blackbirds." *The Kenyon Review*, n.s., 13.4 (1991): 134-35. Print.

—. "Joy Harjo: 'Hieroglyphics [*sic*].'" *YouTube*. Web. 27 May 2009.

Lang, Nancy. "Twin Gods Bending Over." *Poetry and Poetics* 18.3 (1993): 41-49. *JSTOR*. The Society for the Study of the Multi-Ethnic Literature of the United States (MELUS). Web. 21 Mar. 2011.

Scarry, John. "Representing Real Worlds: The Evolving Poetry of Joy Harjo." *World Literature Today, From This World: Contemporary American Indian Literature* 66.2 (1992): 286-91. *JSTOR*. Web. 21 Mar. 2011.

CHAPTER ELEVEN

Michael G. Moran Electronic Portfolio Awards for 2010-2011

Michael G. Moran Awards for 2010-2011

Beginning in 2007, the First-year Composition Program began recognizing the excellent work being done in electronic portfolios for English 1101, 1102, and 1102M by presenting three portfolio awards. Named in honor of Michael G. Moran, a former director of FYC who did much to shape and improve the program and who has continued to support it by serving loyally on the First-year Composition Committee, the awards consist of cash prizes and publication in the *First-year Composition Guide* required of all students registered in our courses and on the FYC site at: http://www. english.uga.edu/newsite/fyc/moran.html.

Brittany Scott's Portfolio	+ - x
📄 How I Fell in Love	Biography
📄 Diary of My Love	Introductory Reflective Essay
📄 For the Love of Art: When Words Fail	Revised Essay 1
📄 For the Love of Speech: When Only Words Prevail	Revised Essay 2
📄 A Heart Transplant	Exhibit of Revision Process
📄 Sharing the Love	Exhibit of Peer Review Process
📄 For the Love of Creation	Wild Card

ENGL 1101

Student: Brittany Scott

Teacher: Christy Desmet

Brittany Scott's ePortfolio is notable for its innovative use of experimental forms and sophisticated personal voice, and perhaps most important, for the strong sense of unity created through her choice of central theme and use of document design.

Unity: Brittany's Biography, entitled "How I Fell in Love," establishes her theme for the entire portfolio. She has chosen to give each exhibit a title related to the theme; she even re-titled her second essay, which is about President Obama's acceptance speech, to fit it smoothly into the thematic sequence. She uses color, typeface, and a consistent page design to create visual connections among the various artifacts; her portfolio also achieves coherence through black-and-white photographs of the author that illustrate each exhibit and chart, in a light-hearted way, her change of attitude over the course of English 1101. Finally, in the Revision Exhibit, Brittany carefully selects examples of problems with diction to illustrate the discussion of that topic in her IRE and explains them in a clear manner by using the language of the Program Grading Rubric and *St. Martin's Handbook*. Brittany chose to use PDF format for her documents in order to ensure perfect display in the web interface.

Innovation: Most striking is the fact that Brittany recasts the Introductory Reflective Essay as a series of diary entries; the Peer Review Exhibit, which chronicles her relationship with classmate "August Mayhem," is also framed unusually, as a narrative that is illustrated with images of the author and of the classmate's chosen image for her essay.

Voice: Brittany's portfolio communicates well with real readers through its authoritative, yet highly personal voice. The portfolio creates a consistent sense of her as a writer and as an individual blessed with intelligence and a sense of humor. Finally, Brittany produced a special Wild Card to fit with her theme: a YouTube video about her poetry that she narrates in her own voice. You can see and listen to the video at YouTube as "Brittany Scott's Wild Card."

HOW I FELL IN **LOVE**

I never knew I would fall in love. I heard people talk about it, but I was never one of the people to stand in near love. In fact, my fear of closeness with love prevented me from ever witnessing the power of love's effect.

Instead, I was a child of hate. I grew up in a house where arguing was a morning ritual, a house where domestic violence was the only quality us kids thought belonged to family. I never searched for love; I always searched for an escape. High and low, I looked. Usually the result was the same nothingness from the day before. For instance, one particular day I took refuge in the basement.

"Where are you going?" My brother yelled at me as I went down to the basement.

The thing is there's nothing in our basement except books and dirty clothes. I wasn't looking for either. I was continuing my search for an escape. But time passed, rather slowly, and the fact that no one came to look for me actually bothered me. So I decided to open one of those many books that were long ago forgotten. I was only nine at the time; therefore, when I picked up Ralph Ellison's *Invisible Man*, I did so only because I felt invisible. I paired the novel with a dictionary and made as much sense of it as I could.

By the age of fourteen I had read the book several times, five years worth of time. And by the age of fifteen I had several authors, several lines of novels, several characters that were embedded in my long term memory as if their lives were my own. In fact, to this day I proclaim that "Battle Royal" from *Invisible Man* is the single best chapter ever written in American literature.

And to this day I admire Ralph Ellison for this intimate chapter that gave me an escape. I admire him for making me fall in love with literature.

REFLECTIVE DIARY OF MY LOVE

I fell in love, and I wanted the world to know. I wanted the world to know about the highs and the lows, about the moments that I never wanted to be over and the moments I never wanted to meet. I wanted to give the inner core of my experience in English 1101. I thought long and hard on the best process to complete this task. I thought about an essay, a short story, a monologue. However, none of them were intimate enough. I wanted to offer the inner depth of my mentality as I flowed through the semester, the imperfections and the insecurities included. After thinking day in and day out, I pondered on this quote I heard by C. Day Lewis: "We do not write in order to be understood, we write in order to understand."

With just that being said, here are my diary entries. Hopefully, they will offer you the same understanding they offered me.

Entry 1: The Honeymoon

Dear Diary,

Me and literature were made for each other. We help define one another. The poetry, plays, novels, short stories, and films that literature offer me help me find sanity in a day-to-day life. In exchange, I offer literature my writing. The combination of the two were born for one another. It's like Catherine Drinker Bowen said, "Writing is not apart from living. Writing is a kind of double living." My double life is the love I have with

literature, with writing, with writing about literature. This love has walked me into an honorable resume, award-winning essays, and publications of poems. I'm pretty sure I can even say that this relationship walked me into the University of Georgia. My test scores were good, my grades were better, but my application essays were AMAZING. I promised my love that I will keep exchanging the gift of my writing with the gift of his presence as long as he never leaves me as I know him. On that day we vowed our love will outlast eternity.

Love,

A Young Writer

Entry 2: The Not So Sweet

Dear Diary,

He's gone as I know him—already. I walked into my first college English class today and received the syllabus—no poems, no plays, no novels. This means no JOHN DONNE, NO SHAKESPEARE, NO TONI MORRISON. This means NO LOVE. I thought we had a deal. Why would he do this to me? He knew how much he meant to me. He knew that all I needed to stay sane was him. And yet, he's gone. My feelings are overwhelming me. I feel as if I am drowning inside a lost love.

But I can't quit yet. I am going to search for my love because I know wherever he is, he is longing for me the way I long for him. I searched for him in my writing. Our first writing assignment was an essay in which we had

to analyze a picture. I thought this was easy. I could simply analyze Oscar Wilde's The Picture of Dorian Grey. . . Again—I was wrong. My teacher actually wanted me to analyze an ordinary picture, no metaphor intended. I left class for the next few weeks with my head hanging low. I felt like I was losing the one thing I had ever found. I felt myself falling out of love with the only thing I had ever loved so passionately and so true.

Love,

An Abandoned Lover

Entry 3: The Silence of Noise

Dear Diary,

Life has to go on. I have to finish school. I HAVE TO. There is not an option in it. Today I thought back to the day when I read that quote by Catherine Drinker Bowen. I lied to you, Diary. I told you that she said "Writing is not apart from living. Writing is a kind of double living." I mean, she did say that. However, I left a part out because I felt like it would never apply to me and my love. I felt like my writing would always be with literature, and literature would always be with me. But since I've been proven wrong, here is the complete quote:

> Writing is not apart from living. Writing is a kind of double living. The writer experiences everything twice. Once in reality and once more in that mirror which waits always before or behind him. So expect to feel both the highs and lows when you're writing.

That mirror is in front and behind me at all times. I know I must address this problem. I must address this issue. My love has fallen down the drain. English class used to be a class in which my top and bottom lip never met each other, because I had so much to say. However, now they are best friends. Now, all the noise that surrounds me in English class is subtle silence that magnifies the warring conflict inside my mind, inside my heart. And when I try to search for him in my writing, it never ends up good. I turned to my poetic style, because it's the most powerful, and because I know he can't ignore it. I make it loud, and sometimes I even forgot that I'm writing prose:

> *Obama says, "It's the answer that led those...to put their hands on the arc of history and bend it once more towards the hope of a better day." These last words of the tricolon turn all the limp hearts into thrusts of force by circling the brittle rim of the audience's brain"*
> *-From Essay 2*

My diction, style, or sentence structure was never fit for any Handbook of St. Martin because all I was interested in was finding my first love. However, through the comments that my teacher left on my essay I could tell that she wanted me to let him go. She felt that it was time to divorce literature and fall in love with my audience. She warranted that my writing style sometimes ignored the factor of audience awareness. She preached clarity, wordiness, word choice... I heard nothing! I figured that those who knew my kind of love, knew that the audience's interpretations weren't the most important, the author's intentions were. They knew that content should outweigh clarity. I figured if this wasn't true, then even Shakespeare would have made some changes. For example, he would have exchanged the blue version of the set of lines from Macbeth with the green, clearer version.

But 'tis strange:

And oftentimes to win us to our harm,

The instruments of darkness tell us truths;

Win us with honest trifles, to betray's

In deepest consequence. *(Act 1 Scene 3 Lines* 1.3.123-27*)*

It's odd

That sometimes, to win us over to the dark side and then do us harm,

That ghosts and witches tell us the truth

And win us with little things, to betray us To greater things.

But of course Shakespeare would have never considered this. And unfortunately I would have never considered saying this to my teacher because she may have failed me for trying to suggest a revision to such an epic writer. I just want her to understand how I feel without my love. I want her to help me find him. I feel she has the power to do that. I'm going to schedule an appointment with her. I'm going to FIND MY FIRST LOVE.

Love,

A Shook Heart

Entry #4: Marriage Counseling

Dear Diary,

The counseling session was simple today. First I explained the problem. I told the counselor how I had a relationship with literature and how this new kind of writing is too new to me because it was not involved with literature. I told her that the reason my essays were filled with metaphors, loaded diction, asyndetons, colloquial language, and excessive imagery is because the subjects I wrote about were not filled with any. I had to invent the creativity, the literary richness, and the irony

because I thought that would bring my love to me. Then I told her how I was wrong. My love and me were still not intimate; therefore, I told her that I wanted to change my major. I told her I feel like I'm in a one way relationship. I'm giving English everything I have, and English is giving me nothing back.

The second part of the counseling session was filled with the counselor telling me how horribly wrong I was. She explained that she enjoys my writing but my excessive intertwining of poetry in prose is distracting. She tried to help me understand that there are two jobs in literature. Writing the words to be analyzed and analyzing the written words. I should never wholly do both. She said I have to find out what it is I love about this relationship I have with literature and let it guide me through the rest.

I left confused. I'm still confused. My mind is full of so many questions. I need to go back to the core. What it is that I really love? Is it Ralph Ellison? Is it literature? Is it poetry? Is it figurative language? I feel like I will never know. I feel like my love is too foreign to know where it initially aroused from.

Love,
A Searching Lover

Entry #5: Redefining My Love

Dear Diary,

This morning I woke up with answers, soothing answers. I chased my falling in love back to the roots. I did not fall in love with literature, exactly. I did not wholly fall in love with poetry or figurative language, either. These are all branches that the stem of my love grew into. However, the true thing I fell in love with was not as specific as any of these things. What I fell in love with was the single most impressive nature of Ralph Ellison's Invisible Man. I fell in love with the art  *of creation. I fell in love with the imagination it takes to think of an idea, the intellect it takes to build a plot, and the poetic language it takes to translate such plots into words. And while my love for the creation around me grew, I fell in love with my own creation. I fell in love with my ability to put black on white—pen to paper. I fell in love with the fact that my creations began to create themselves. I can think and my brain would write for itself. I can look and my mind would read for itself. This is what I fell in love with, something rooted so deep in literature that I begin to mistake their faces for one another.*

However, now I know the true face of my lover. And I know that he never left me. Because as long as I could write, read, and interpret creation was with me. In fact, the underlying connection between my three essays was based on my love for creation. The two essays used for my portfolio, "For the Love of Art" and "For the Love of Speech," both explore creation at its best. The first explores the art of creating a captivating painting, and the second explores the creation of a meaningful speech. Both the painting and the speech analyzed portray some degree of mixing poetry with rhetoric—a beautiful creation. Even my third essay, "Mending Blindness," is a piece analyzing the creation of a influential song. My love was so close this whole time. Shame on me for thinking he left.

Love,

A Young Writer

Brittany Scott

English 1101

Dr.Desmet

Fall 2010

When Words Fail

Make a glance last a lifetime: This is the primary goal of artists. Tracing back to Leonardo DaVinci during the Renaissance Era, one of the ultimate purposes of art has always been to create a piece so eloquent that the elements of the artwork tell a story themselves (Atsma). Hence, in this form art relays a message, making it a definite form of literature. As literature, art is a tool to bring about social awareness, consciousness of history, and/or aesthetic appreciation. Kenneth Vann reveals his familiarity with art as a tool of expression. When asked how his works benefit him personally, Vann explains that "his artwork gives [him] a means to express an idea that [he] can't find the words to say." A notable example of such artistic expression by Vann is his painting *The Fight*. In this piece, Kenneth Vann uses eclectic details with rhetorical incongruities to present the internal struggles for self-worth that African Americans endure and to furthermore provide aesthetic social commentary, which highlights the fact that Blacks' concurrent mission to find equality and freedom in America is still highly incomplete.

Without any application of a deep analysis, one major detail is easily digested by Vann's audience. That detail is African Americans in America. History proves that the entire process of Americanization for African Americans was a struggle. Dated back to 1619, when African Americans first stepped foot in America, the "fight" was in progress. According to Darlene Hines, Africans' first business in America was their positions as indentured servants (Hines 282). However, in only a few years this willingness was taken full advantage of. As America's greed grew, the need for servants grew. And soon, "the willingness of indentured servitude grew into the helplessness of slavery" (Hines 283). The rule was simple; if your mom was black, then you were black, and if you were black, then you were a slave (Hines 283). Hines explains that by the 1700s, ninety percent of all African Americans were building what we know today as the land of milk and honey (299). They spent two centuries turning America into one of the Industrial Revolution's prosperous countries and turning American factories into the most appealing trade market of the globe. Thus, one concludes that African Americans helped shape America and the nation's abilities around the globe with their bare hands, on their bare knees—literally.

Such knowledge about the early journey of African Americans in America is needed for any true analysis of Kenneth Vann's image. This information is the foundation of the oppression that the image depicts: Vann states that his image "symbolizes the seemingly everlasting struggle of the black community" (Woods 15). The history's significance also derives from the fact that the creator himself "is an African American History and Art major at Howard University" (Woods 13).Therefore, his intellectual and cultural connection with the struggle of African Americans allow him to deeply explore it in his painting. With this one painting, Vann portrays the overall conflict African Americans face, an internal conflict of historical and cyclical significance. The internal battle can be seen by simply focusing on the three subjects. Each of the subjects reflects a historical aesthetic piece that assists Vann in emphasizing the inner issues of all African Americans—specifically, the three major stems of the struggle for the last two centuries: self-regard, civil rights, and emancipation.

This fight within is first depicted by the man on the left. His head is completely back. His arms are slightly outstretched, and his muscles are being strained. This posture allows Vann to give off the impression that this man is a reflection of Jesus Christ, for Jesus is drawn and sculpted this way on more than one occasion. Such examples include Nivardus of Milon's painting entitled *The Crucifixion* and James Tiscot's eighteenth century painting entitled *Jesus Praying*. As with Jesus and Christianity, the man's prayers are for the society around him; he is praying that they change

their ways and perceptions. Also as Jesus was on the cross, the subject is helpless and hopeless in the hands of society. He is begging for help from a higher source. He is in need of an answer, for a change.

Similarly to the man on the left, the man in the middle's posture directly resembles another famous work of art. The man is kneeling and holding a globe in Vann's attempt to recreate Cardinal Alessandro Farnese's sculpted Greek Titan, Atlas. In Homer's *The Odyssey,* Atlas symbolizes

 endurance (Atsma). Specifically, he is labeled the one who "knows the depth of all the sea" (*Odyssey,* i.52.). However, because he leads a group of Titans to rebel against Zeus, the Gods place the world upon his shoulders as punishment. In relation to Atlas, the symbolism of Vann's subject's posture lies in the fact that for hundreds of years, African Americans did nothing more than build America from soil and lead America to prosperity with production; when they rebelled, they were punished. Consequently, the inner deconstruction of this unjust lifestyle still cages their minds and souls. The mental destruction is a burden that they struggle to uplift off their backs still.

Likewise, the woman on the right has her hands held up to the sky, mimicking the *Statue of Liberty*. With the torch in her hand, she is showing desperation for a better day and begging for enlightenment—which is what the statue's torch truly symbolizes. She needs the light to outshine the expected ignorance of her culture and to light the way of their lives' dark path.

In addition to the figures' symbolic body positions, certain contrasts in the image also provide enlightening details regarding the psychological aspect of African Americans. For instance, all of the subjects' appearances contrast with the colorfulness of the image. Their dull faces do not match or complement the bright background; this further emphasizes the fact that it is "their struggle." The rest of America will proceed to go with the wind, as the flag attempts to do in the image, without paying any mind to African Americans. Furthermore, the muscular build of the subjects, in contrast with their straining and indistinguishable faces, further underscores the African American psyche. This obvious discomfort of the subjects reveals their awkwardness in the midst of society, but their muscular frame shows their progress inside their own fight. They are not free of trials; instead, they are getting stronger. As Vann states while explaining the title of his image *The Fight*, "There's a factor that people do not realize about African Americans; it is the fact that they are progressing in a struggle, not struggling to progress. African Americans are not even a century out of the nadir [lowest point], their minds hold personal low worth" (Woods 14). Vann explains that the subjects are "progressing in a struggle." However, they have yet to completely overcome the strife. And as a result of the subjects' lack of sufficiency in gaining complete victory, they lack identity. The subjects' virtual facelessness and lack of direct eye-contact reiterate Vann's idea of this incomplete battle and such mental low worth.

One of the main issues that accompany these internal battles and prove that African Americans are still struggling is their lack of equality in America. Obviously, this issue is not as bad as it was when Jim Crow was widespread in the South. But Vann made a point to show that the issue still exists. The presentation of inequality is hidden in a few of his image's incongruities. The most apparent examples are the figures' nakedness and near nakedness. This inappropriate exposure adds to Blacks' inability to properly belong in America. Judged by appearance, this ten percent of America's population stands out in a humiliating, vulnerable, burdensome way. Alongside this detail of their outcast nature is the fact that the flag is pinned down. Vann establishes ultimate irony in this one detail. A free-flying flag is pinned down. A flag is representative of who the people of a country are, of what the people believe in, and what the people stand for. However, this flag does not fly equally over all citizens. Therefore, African Americans have to pin it down to fully grasp any wholeness of America. They have to fight, as the title suggests, to get the feeling of a true citizen.

This idea of inequality is further expressed with the most dynamic factor in the image, the globe. Usually a globe is blue and green, both lively colors. More importantly, blue and green represent the resources provided by the natural Earth. Contrarily, the globe in Vann's image is black and brown. These somber colors highlight the limited resources and the virtual economic powerlessness of African Americans. Apparently, Blacks do not have equal opportunities. The bright possibilities that the natural world offers the vast majority of American society are dull improbabilities to African Americans.

Alongside the issue of inequality is African Americans' lack of freedom, which Vann underscores with the Statue of Liberty that is kept separate from the subjects due to the American flag, which divides the subjects and the statue. This provides social commentary on the fact that America keeps African Americans away from full emancipation. Moreover, Vann precisely makes sure certain details on the Statue of Liberty are hidden. One of these details is the broken shackles that are on the real Statue of Liberty's feet. This underscores the idea that African Americans' shackles are not broken. They are still somehow morally or politically or economically or socially or racially enslaved.

Art captures a moment and makes it momentous. Kenneth Vann does not try to revive history in his image. He is, instead, trying to tell the world that the fight of African Americans, respected as history, is still present. He allows history to enhance art and creates a pivotal masterpiece. His selective artistic and historic elements weave his artwork into a voice that evocatively comments on the lives and struggles of African Americans. This voice, created with oil paints and pastel, is gentle enough to seek pity, yet dynamic enough to reap change in awareness. And that is the importance of a piece of art, to leave the audience with a different or enlightened perspective. Vann allows his picture to provide the enlightenment that has many times been offered to society: "Black people have always been apart of the American nation that they helped to build, but they have also been a nation unto themselves with their own experiences, struggles, and aspirations" (Du Bois, qtd. in Hines). However, Vann's enlightenment seemingly offers a more captivating presentation and literary richness than the average writers who portray the same theme. This difference can be summed up into one contrasting factor: "They use their pen, [he] uses [his] paintbrush" (Woods 13).

Works Cited

Atsma, J Aaron. "Theoi Project." *Theoi Greek Mythology: Exploring Greek Mythology in Classical Literature and Art.* Aaron J. Atsma, n.d. Web. 18 August 2010.

Hines, Darlene Clark. *The African-American Odyssey*. Vol 2. San Francisco: Kelleman, 2001. Print. 2 vols.

Homer. *The Odyssey*. Trans. Robert Fagles. New York: Viking, 1996. Print.

Tiscot, James. *Jesus Praying*. 17th Century. Bible Art of Brooklyn Museum. New York Creative Commons. 2009. Web. 24 Nov. 2010

Woods, Kyra. "Hot Mindz: Kenneth Vann." *The Unspoken* May. 2009: 13-16. Print.

Brittany Scott

English 1101

Dr. Desmet

Fall 2010

When Only Words Prevail

On November 4, 2008 at 11:13 p.m, change came to America. The 2008 election had been finalized; for the first time in history, America elected an African American president. For the first time since Roosevelt, the Democratic Party won by a land slide. For the first time to many, history became personal as Barack Hussein Obama walked onto the Chicago stage to accept his position as President-elect of the United States. As James Wood said, "many of us would have watched in tears if President-elect Obama had only thanked his campaign staff and shuffled off to bed, but his midnight address was written in a language with roots and stirred in his audience a correspondingly deep emotion" (Wood). Obama uses this speech to rebuild the morality and social state of a nation blinded by the fire of despair. His rhetoric and oratorical mastery allow him to begin the reconstruction of the people who matter most, the citizens. With such skills, Barack Obama not only empowers and unites his nation by strengthening their belief in the possibility of progressive change and their hope, but he also places himself on a pedestal near two great men whose style and focus he shadows, Abraham Lincoln and Dr. Martin Luther King Jr, thus making him even more potent as a leader and speaker.

Barack Obama's first notable invention in his speech is what inevitably makes the audience reach an ultimate intensity—the arrangement. Instead of organizing his address in a manner where introduction leads to proposal, Obama orders his speech in a way that gains his audience's support and passion as the speech unfolds. First, he focuses on and moves through the people as did Dr. Martin Luther King in many of his speeches (Warren). Then, he floats through time and history to focus on the future of the nation. With such a strategic order, Obama asserts that the fate of the future is a product of the citizens' strength and unity, echoing Lincoln's description of America as a place "of the people, by the people, and for the people" (Hines 1). Thus, the full efficacy of Obama's speech is only seen when it is analyzed in parts, sectioned by this same strategic arrangement.

Barack Obama's initial interests are his nation and those who have lost faith in America. Obama's speech addresses their mentality in a demanding manner, a separate but equal manner. This is done by using parallelism. He calls attention to she or he "who still doubts" and she or he "who still wonders" and she or he "who still questions." He juxtaposes these three groups because similarly they are *all* uncertain of the power of the nation. Furthermore, Obama places all of them beside each other to show that they are *all* equally wrong. He succinctly responds to these minds full of doubt and questions by declaring, "Tonight is [their] answer." His being elected refutes their doubtful beliefs because he, the person who "was never the likeliest candidate," is President-elect. If the country can reap such election results, then there is no need to question the nation's existing power.

However, this "answer" is only one part of a tricolon (repetition consisting of three parts of increasing power) that assists Obama in truly empowering his nation. The tricolon continues to describe the answer as "the answer told by lines stretched around schools" and "the answer told by young and old, rich and poor, democratic and republic." Nevertheless, the tricolon is completed by its fourth addition. Obama states, "It's the answer that led those who have been so cynical and fearful and doubtful... to put their hands on the arc of history and bend it once more towards the hope of a better day." This last line, serving as a rhetorical climax, turns the skeptical citizens into believers. The power of this line comes from its climax-engendering position in the tricolon and "the arc" resembling Dr. Martin Luther King's phrase stating that "the arc of the moral universe is long but it bends towards justice" (Wood). Obama introduces an ethical appeal as he gains his audience's trust by letting them know he is finishing what King started, thereby making them feel safe under his leadership. This security induces comfort and confidence in the audience, which strengthens their dynamism.

Extending this emphasis of the dynamic power of the nation, Obama later employs logical appeals. He provides the audience with information which highlights the strength of a united democracy. He states that the lines of voters were "in numbers never seen," and that voters waited in lines for "three to four hours." Many voters also were voting for the first time in their lives. All of these details lead to the multiplication of the power Obama is referring to. The fact that Obama won 367 electoral votes to McCain's 173, the fact that 67 million of the 120 million votes were for Obama, and the fact that America had more voters in the 2008 election than ever before in history underscores the power Obama is referring to (Hines 662). The potency that exists in America already enables the nation, as a united people, to do the unthinkable. Obama simply wants his audience to tap into the potential embedded in the country in order to do more.

Having empowered his nation, Obama goes back to the roots of his campaign—change. Obama introduces emotional appeals as he makes his audience feel superior by declaring that they are "above all" and by dedicating his election victory to them. He furthers this pathos by bringing attention to the conditions under which the victory began. Using comparisons to construct an emotional connection with his audience, Obama distinguishes his election from the conventional election by asserting that the victory was not "hatched" in the halls of Washington. With this one term he exemplifies the fact that this triumph did not just come to life in the blink of an eye or the crack of an egg. Instead, it was formed "in the backyards of Des Moines, and the living rooms of Concord, and the back porches of Charleston." Instead, it was built by "5 dollars" here and "10 dollars" there and "20 dollars" when possible. This sad story is not drawn to seek pity, though: it adds to the possibility for progress, the logic that is introduced next. He explains that his election, his step-by-step and prayer-by-prayer election, was indeed one "by the people," thus dedicating the rebirth of true democracy to the audience.

As a result, Obama introduces his main argument; based on the nation's previous accomplishments while united, one must assume that possibilities are endless if the nation is united. If one less fortunate campaign team can fight through "the bitter cold and scorching heat" to build a million dollar team of winners, then an entire nation can surely rebuild a country "block by block, brick by brick, calloused hand by calloused hand."

Obama continues to combine rhetorical appeals and techniques to persuade his nation to believe in change and unity. He brings attention to the fact that his election "alone is not the change we seek. It is only the chance for us to make that change." He then comments on the "enormity of the task that lies ahead." He sums it up into "two wars, a planet in peril, the worst financial crisis in a century." The aysndeton (lack of conjunctions) allows Obama to emphasize that the problems are all separate issues for America and that none of them outweighs the other. More importantly, it lessens the load of the task by making it seem like three minor issues instead of one major issue and consequently brings comfort to the audience. This comfort is furthered by an ethical appeal, the term "we." Obama's phrase "We, as a people, will get there," is a quote from Martin Luther King's "I've Been to the Mountaintop" (Warren). This fact adds an extra degree of sincerity and unity. If one was wondering how Obama would or could do anything, this incorporation of King's words offers the ethos that erases their doubt. The nation feels that they can get there. Despite the fact that "the roads ahead will be long" and that "the climb will be steep," they will seek change. The "roads" of America will no longer diverge, the nation will climb the mountain of prosperity and progress as a whole, as a "we." Suitably, his election is the most apparent example of that. His being elected helps prove that change is a plausible and possible and probable thing.

Obama starts another ethical appeal in an effort to further unify his nation. He reaches out to his audience by explaining to them that he can't make it without them, that change "can't happen" without them. He seeks to touch the people who are so doubtful of change that they don't even support it. He addresses them as those whose support he has "yet to earn." As a humble man, he not only asks for their help but tells them that "[he] will be [their] President too." Obama shows that he is ready for change; he is only waiting on his nation to join him. More importantly, at this point Obama speaks as if Lincoln's ghost lives inside of him (Wood). He alludes to Lincoln to certify the possibility of change and to, moreover, highlight the probability of change when a nation is united. This is a main idea in Lincoln's first and second inauguration speeches, along with his Gettysburg Address (Hines 701). Obama shows his knowledge of Lincoln as he carefully "crafted his language, reminiscent of Lincoln's appeal for unity and reason, to encourage Americans to embrace change and hope" (Hines 698). Furthermore, he uses the extra worth gained from his evocative style to proclaim "the true genius of America": America can be perfected; "America can change."

After uniting his citizens and gaining their faith in change, Obama focuses on the hope of his nation. He reintroduces his renowned campaign slogan, "Yes We Can," a motto of faith in possibilities (Zeleny). He rests his motto on the belief that "what we've already achieved gives us HOPE for what we can and must achieve tomorrow." The audience becomes emotionally charged as he repeats "Yes We Can" after every section of the testimony. Each time the phrase is chanted, the volume of the audience increases. Such rising intensity underscores the audience's rapidly growing degree of hope. In response, Obama allows logic to create a final mark. He takes his audience (which is now united, empowered, and supportive of change) and conquers any future doubt by using Ann Nixon Cooper's testimony to influence them to find the bravery of having hope. This 106 year old woman witnessed an evolving world in America. The many changes she has seen through her life allow him to provide examples of growth, such as Woman's Suffrage and the Civil Rights Movement. As a result, Obama points out that the probability of refinement occurring is high because of the pattern of change that occurred so much in the past. Therefore, Americans not only have "unyielding hope" as an emotional concept, but also as a logical matter.

The power of rhetoric can greatly move a people. Barack Obama's speech is the perfect demonstration of such power in effect. His words are enlightening, captivating, and influential. He does not simply rely on persuasion to make his audience believe in his optimistic view; instead, he employs rhetoric to guide his audience in building their *own* positive perspective. Even more significantly, he rides on the beliefs of his historical predecessors. Obama brings forth an assertiveness that is reinforced by Dr. Martin Luther King as he speaks of reclaiming the "dream," and Abraham Lincoln as he speaks of reaffirming the "fundamental truth, that...we are one." With this credit of being a glowing shadow of King and Lincoln and placing his focus on making change, Obama uses this "defining moment" as a chance to redefine his nation. He binds the wounds crippling his nation and leaves his audience faithful for prosperity—faithful for him.

Works Cited

"Barack Obama wins presidential election." CNN. 4 November 2008. 6 November 2008. http://:www.cnn.com/2008/ politics/11/04election.president/index.html. November 5, 2008.

Hines, Darlene Clark. *The African-American Odyssey*. Vol 2. San Francisco: Kelleman, 2001. Print. 2 vols.

Warren, Mervyn A. *King Came Preaching: The Pulpit Power of Dr. Martin Luther King, Jr.* Chicago: InterVarsity Press, 2001. Print.

Wood, James. "Close Reading: Victory Speech." *The New Yorker*. Conde Nest Digital. 2010. 17 November 2008. http://www. newyorker.com/talk/2008/11/17/081117ta_talk_wood.

Zeleny, Jeff. "Obama Clinches Nomination; First Black Candidate to Lead a Major Party Ticket." *The New York Times* 4 June 2008: A8. Print.

A HEART TRANSPLANT

As an English major in love with the subject, the revision process is the most important skill I will learn as a student. The skills of editing an essay effectively will ease my heartaches through the first four years of my relationship with the subject. Usually, by the time my stylistic writing and imagination take control of my thoughts, my thoughts are lost. Consider the point of the essay to be my heart. Consider the poetic nature of my style to be the sweetness of sugars. Now consider the sum of **HEART+SUGAR+SUGAR+SUGAR**[1101] **+SUGAR**. Despite the fact that science is not my strong point, it is easy to see that the sum of this equation is one thing—**HEART ATTACK**. The problem is that I write with all my heart. But too much of anything is bad. And too much gloss in an essay leads to one sugar-plated presentation that the audience will choose not to read. Therefore, the main issue I had with my writing was clarity, appropriate language, and wordiness. The end effect of an essay full of these issues suggests that I am seemingly unaware of my audience, the desired coherence of an essay, and the expected presentation of a good essay. Nevertheless, the distinction of my authoritative and compelling voice can be respectfully recognized only if I incorporate it in the proper manner. The process of this modification of my style is what I call the Heart Transplant. The following process is a step-by-step view of my revision method to fit this manner. All examples are from Paper 3, Video Analysis of Rascal Flatt's song "Skin." This essay analyzed the compositional choice of the song's lyrics and video. Mostly, I focused on the effect the group made on the audience. The color codes represent discrepancies of clarity, language, and wordiness, respectively. The revised version is labeled in pink.

1. *This particular sentence was crediting the group, providing ethical appeal for my audience by showing the group's charity ties.*

> **They are known for** endless **charitable efforts,** which include
> their being spokespersons for the Hendersonville Jason
> Foundation, their working as celebrity ambassadors for
> the American Red Cross, and their on-going work with the
> Monroe Carell Children's Hospital.

The term "endless" is a hyperbole in this sentence and it makes me sound as if I'm praising the band. I do not need to praise the band; my readers know they are important because I am writing about them—period. Also, the term is more potent than the object of the preposition "for." That is a problem because I want the audience to know that the band does charitable deeds, not that they have a never ending amount of deeds. A sufficient change is to replace the term "endless" with "many."

The other issue in this sentence is the clarity in the parallel structure. The attempted parallelism is ineffective because the items in the series are not in parallel grammatical form. Instead of each phrase being a gerund or noun phrase, they vary. Thus, a sufficient change is to make each series begin with a gerund.

> **They are known for** many **charitable efforts,** which include
> being spokespersons for the Hendersonville Jason Foundation,
> working as celebrity ambassadors for the American Red Cross,
> and working with the Monroe Carell Children's Hospital

---

2. *This sentence was analyzing two scenes that the group paralleled throughout the video.*

> **As Sara Beth psychologically** distances herself with
> surrounding people, **she mentally finds relief in her dreams.**

The first issue of clarity occurs with the inappropriate idiom usage of "with surrounding people." This is unidiomatic, because to the American ear this phrase means that Sarah Beth distances herself and takes the surrounding people with her. However, that is not my intended meaning. Therefore, I must use the word "from" instead of "with." This will show that Sarah Beth goes away from her neighbors.

As Sara Beth psychologically distances herself from surrounding people, **she mentally finds relief in her dreams.**

---

3. This example is a sentence describing one of the characters in the video.

The boy arrives at her house and to everyone's surprise he has a new hair cut—a bald cut resembling the average cancer patient undergoing chemotherapy.

The error in this sentence is the illogical comparison between the bald cut and a cancer patient. Comparisons must be made between items that are alike; otherwise my audience will be distracted. In this instance, my audience may be left wondering if the boy had a cancer patient tattooed on his head. In order to be clear I have to compare the boy's bald cut to the bald cut of most cancer patients.

The boy arrives at her house and to everyone's surprise he has a new hair cut—a bald cut resembling the baldness of an average cancer patient undergoing chemotherapy.

---

4. This example was of a section used to elaborate on the symbolism provided by the inclusion of dancers in the video.

> **Additionally, the slow and flowing movements of the dancers represent the placid and free lifestyle Sara Beth dreams of. She dreams of being free from worrying and suffering. She dreams of her hair blowing like the dancers' hair, and a glowing beauty like they have.**

The wordiness occurs in this sentence because I include sentences and phrases that I do not have to include. This interrupts the flow of my essay, which distracts from my essay's coherent form. Instead of the babbling, I can easily insert punctuation to reduce clauses to phrases and to reduce phrases to single words. This will ultimately improve the fluency of my essay.

> **Additionally, the slow and flowing movements of the dancers represent the placid and free lifestyle Sara Beth dreams of, free from worry and suffering. She dreams of having the dancers' blowing hair and glowing beauty.**

As the editor inside me takes over, examples like this become a book full. I read my paper out loud, act as if I'm my audience, act as if I had just read fifteen other papers...I basically do everything possible to make sure my paper is distinct and clear at the same time. I'm sure I'm not the first to admit the process of editing and rearranging is about four times longer than the process of inventing. However, for satisfaction...it's all worth it!

SHARING THE LOVE

August Mayhem is, overall, a mature, profound writer. Her well-rounded knowledge always guides her to writing provocative essays. However, she is a process writer: her knowledge many times leaves her thoughts scattered and jumbled. The content is always present; however, the knowledge is not always thesis-driven. Therefore, her papers begin off as thoughts, on top of thoughts, on top of shrugs of uncertainties. My main job as her peer editor is to make sure August begins her paper and that the paper evolves into an essay with a theoretical thesis. This takes a complete understanding of August's intentions and the subject she is writing about. Therefore, the first step of my peer revision is calling August to see exactly what she is trying to prove in her essay. **Next, I assist her in organizing her thoughts to build a thesis-driven essay.** Lastly, I show my respect for St. Martin and edit her essay for grammatical purposes, particularly checking for the most common mistakes.

THE PHONE CALL

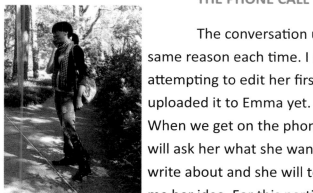

The conversation usually takes place for the same reason each time. I call her because while attempting to edit her first draft, I realized she had not uploaded it to Emma yet. When we get on the phone, I will ask her what she wants to write about and she will tell me her idea. For this particular  example, she wanted to write an analytical essay on the cover of a VOGUE magazine. I was familiar with the magazine, so I could help her brainstorm. Also, August had a strong foundation of information in history and fashion. Therefore, a picture like the one to the right was of her comfort zone. By the end of the conversation, August and I had developed a descriptive purpose for her paper. In her essay, August was to explain how the image attracts readers and creates controversy regarding stereotypes.

ORGANIZATION OF THOUGHTS (August's *introduction is used for this example*)

DRAFT 2:

This VOGUE cover features Gisele Bündchen and LeBron James for the "Shape Issue". The photo was taken by Annie Lebovitz, who is known for her beautiful but controversial work. This image displays both of these sides by mixing the expected and unexpected, and bringing politics through fashion. It us an elegantly posed and vibrant image animating the topics of the issue and making the reader want to delve into the fashion, while also stirring up controversy by depicting stereotypes.

A PIECE OF MY HEART: **Overall, August's ideas were present and intriguing. However, as an introduction, this paragraph must engage the reader and introduce the subject in a manner that allows the audience to build expectations for the rest of the essay. I told August she needs to implement my side comments and add needed sentences to increase the fluency of her paragraph. She must also include more background information to explain the controversial idea she is referring to in the thesis. In regards to being coherent, August should make sure she relates her arguments to VOGUE"S audience; she should add a detail explaining how the audience would react to the controversy the cover creates.**

PROOF READING *(this example includes my suggested changes)*

DRAFT 2:

When VOGUE came out with their annual "Shape Issue" in 2008, they chose basketball player LeBron James and supermodel Giselle Bündchen for the cover. The two seem to be the perfect fit for the issue focusing on model physique and athletic bodies, as they are among the most successful and well known in their respective careers. However, the pair's stance stirred up the fashion and political world over its similarities to old King Kong images. The photo was taken by Annie Leibovitz, who is known for her beautiful and controversial work. This image displays both of these sides by mixing the expected and unexpected, and bringing together politics and fashion. The cover goes beyond just shape. It is an elegantly posed and vibrant image animating the topics of the issue and making the reader want to delve into the fashion, while also stirring up controversy by depicting stereotypes, and making the reader take a second look at their view on these issues.

A PIECE OF MY HEART: August made a great improvement in content. However, I explained to her that she needs to make the necessary grammatical changes to her essay so that the presentation and design of her essay are enhanced. Also, many of her sentences begin with pronouns. I advised her to vary her sentence types and structure before the final draft.

FOR THE LOVE OF CREATION

I admitted that I was in love with Creation. I must also admit that out of all the things that creation enables—poetry is my favorite. Poetry is the best reflection of my love story with creativity. It truly defines who I am. Therefore, for my Wild Card I decided to include a piece of poetry. The film is humorous, for a comic relief. However, the voice-over is the presentation of my poem entitled "Creation." The poem explains my basic process of writing a poem. Click the following link to enjoy: http://www.youtube.com/watch?v=aRY3g1YOGM8.

Taylor Stark's Portfolio	+ - x
Biography	Biography Download
IRE Essay	Introductory Reflective Essay Download
Revised Essay 1	Revised Essay 1 Download
Revised Essay 2	Revised Essay 2 Download
Revision Exhibit	Exhibit of Revision Process Download
Peer Review	Exhibit of Peer Review Process Download
Wildcard	Wild Card Download

ENGL1102

Student: Taylor Stark

Teacher: Caroline Young

... it's living that makes me want to write, not reading — although it's reading that makes me love writing.

— *Eudora Welty*

Taylor Stark's ePortfolio offers a compelling portrait of the author as both a person and a writer. The format of the ensemble is simple, focusing on careful analysis and details of literary language.

Writer's ethos: Taylor's portfolio portrays the author as thoughtful, attentive to self and others, and as caring deeply about writing as a vehicle for thought and feeling. (Perhaps it is no surprise that Taylor's instructor, like her student, is a creative writer.) Taylor's ethos is projected through not only what she says, but how she says it. She has a characteristic prose style with easy flow and precise diction that give added "punch" to her reflections and analysis. To get a sense of Taylor's style, you might look at the last paragraph of her Introductory Reflective Essay (the term "grammatical mishap" is particularly wonderful) or the first paragraph of Revised Essay 1, which is notable for its easy "flow."

Unity: Taylor's portfolio also has a subtle unity that is based on the fluid relationship of analytic and lyrical writing, of poetry and prose. The title of the first essay, "Fabrication to Freedom," characterizes the whole portfolio. Both of Taylor's revised essays, which are the centerpiece of the portfolio, deal with song lyrics; at the same time, both deal with the portfolio's overarching themes of growth and the imaginative journey offered by literature. The portfolio concludes with an original poem that echoes the sentiments and diction of the Biography (look, for instance, at the use of the word "vicarious").

Craft: To support her ethos as a writer, Taylor offers strong testimony of her attention to writerly craft. As a committed writer, for instance, she recognizes the uses of such activities as peer review in helping with her own writing; and her Peer Review and Revision Exhibits show through multiple examples that she consistently revises and edits with care both her own and her peers' work.

Biography

Original thought. If possible, it does not come about by mimicking the ideas and creations of other beings. If impossible, one should at least live as if it is so, as to stay clear of the vicarious life. I was once a victim of this fatal disease, but then my eyes were abruptly opened to the realization that life is better spent living than observing. The individual I am today has been carefully sculpted by magnificent moments, tragic experiences,

... it's living that makes me want to write, not reading — although it's reading that makes me love writing.

— Eudora Welty

profound people and my humble roots. It is all about growth. Through each conversation, each image of nature, each melody and each spoken word, I am taking in more and more knowledge. What I will choose to do with that wisdom is unknown, but whatever I decide, it is a step. A step in a direction and that path will lead me somewhere. My past roads and destinations do not define me, but rather my reactions to them uncover who I really am. Often times it takes static to acknowledge motion, death to know life, war to feel peace, lost to be found and misjudgment to be certain. I am an amateur explorer. I seek to grab life and to live it without expectation. What I have and will stumble upon will become the blueprints of my outward expression. It makes sense you know, what good does hoarding all my adventures do me? My travels do not vanish from my hands when whispered into another's ear. The greatest aspect is that what I have done will never be undone and what I will do is waiting for me in an abyss of uncertainty.

Introductory Reflective Essay

My mind has always tempted me to break through the boundaries involved in the composition of traditional essays. In my high school English classes, I was bored with the standard Commentary-and-Key Passage required writings because I felt as if my voice could not be conveyed. My junior year, I discovered journalism. Immediately, I found my niche in the Opinions section of our newspaper. Through this outlet, I could write about anything my heart desired, as I was not constrained by format, typical sentence structure, and a conventional teacher. When I came to the University of Georgia as an English Major, I was hit with the daunting realization that I would soon be immersed in writing and analysis once again. My fear was that my personal expression would have to be sacrificed in order to receive an acceptable grade in my class. Little did I know, my English 1102 classroom experience would challenge me in a way that encouraged my style of writing to flourish.

In our first major writing assignment, we were asked to analyze a song that parallels our life and incorporate both aspects into our paper. If there is one thing I love as much as writing, it is music. I knew exactly what I wanted to say, but I had no earthly idea how to intertwine a song into my thoughts. In the past I would have given the paper my best attempt and turned it in, hoping I accomplished what the prompt asked for. However, our class requires students to turn in several drafts of our essay as stepping-stones to our final draft. This concept was not entirely new to me, since I had been an editor for the newspaper, but it had never been a part of my English courses. For the first time, I had not only one pair of eyes looking over my paper, but my professor's and my classmates' as well. This brought to light issues in my writing that I had simply skipped over. The writing process for this paper allowed me to come closer to my full potential, but also, the topic provoked a sense of intrigue in me. In my portfolio, I have included this first essay as my "Revised Essay 1." I did so to display my successful integration of song analysis into my personal account. This first essay is also a transition into my "Revised Essay 2" because it shows my development from one prompt to another while still maintaining my individuality as a writer.

As the semester progressed, I began to understand that my voice could be heard in my writing, even if the subject was not myself. In our last paper, we were told to analyze the soundtrack of a film. If there is anything I love as much as writing and music, it is film. First, I chose a familiar soundtrack that interprets the actions and dialogue on screen. The key to this paper was to balance the plot and the analysis of the underlying soundtrack as they walk hand and hand throughout the film. I picked this paper as my "Revised Essay 2" to demonstrate my progression as a writer. At first, I found it very difficult to formulate appropriate descriptions of the background musical accompaniments to *Stranger Than Fiction*, but as I thought of the feelings the music provoked within me, it all fell into place. Since I was able to write about material that resonated with my passions and impacted me personally, I found that analyzing the film was more effortless than I expected. That same voice illustrated in my "Revised Essay 1" is still present, but the difference is that my style emerges when analyzing someone else's material.

I have come to the conclusion that my writing will never be perfect. It will never reach its full potential because growth is a continual process. Before this semester, I thought I could only write creatively when my writing did not concern my school assignments. I have come to the understanding that I can utilize that foundation to unpack meanings and analyze other writers' work while allowing my "original thoughts" to intrigue my audience. I may still find the occasional misspelling or grammatical mishap, but I am much more confident in my ability as a versatile writer. My portfolio is a depiction of the evolution I have undergone in order to reach the current state of mind I am in. Now, I optimistically forge ahead, without expectation, so that I may embrace and apply whatever else the writing world has in store for me.

Taylor Stark

Ms. Young

English 1102

17 November 2010

Fabrication to Freedom

As a young child, I resided "in an old house in Paris that was covered in vines" with eleven other rambunctious girls. When I was eleven, I accidentally stumbled upon the magical land of Narnia while venturing into an old wardrobe during an innocent game of hide and seek. Since then, I have unearthed numerous conspiracies, and I have sailed the seven seas. I was taught the art of beekeeping by the Boatwright sisters, and I learned the significance of the overlooked pronoun "I." At the end of a typical day, I would stand on my balcony and look out over the water to focus my gaze on a single, flashing green light at the end of a familiar dock. In the past couple of years, I have lived the life of a lonely traveling salesman, inhabited a small town where nothing remarkable ever takes place, witnessed both sides of European imperialism in Africa, and opened my drowsy eyelids to find myself transformed into a gigantic insect. In retrospect, my life has been anything but dull. However, I cannot claim these outrageous happenings as my own personal journey because in fact, they are not mine at all.

Since I can remember, my nose has been wedged between two pages and my eyes have adjusted to fine print. Whether it was a Dr. Seuss book, classic novel or a *New York Times* bestseller, I fully immersed myself in whatever type of literature I could get my hands on. Reading was never a chore or just another mundane class assignment; it was in my blood. The art of fiction transported me to a fantasy world that I could control. The local bookstore was my sweet shop, each aisle filled with hundreds of distinct dreams that I could fall into with just one turn of a page. Corresponding to this unreal sense, the song *Dream* by Priscilla Ahn conveys a childhood into adulthood transition that is prompted by a little girl's love of dreaming. The images, diction, and themes incorporated to emphasize the progression of the persona's life in the song mirror my own personal journey from a life of fabrication to one of authentic freedom. In the second and third lines of the song, the speaker describes her childhood playtime when she says, "alone in my little world / who dreamed of a little home for me." The specific diction "alone" (l. 2) reveals her isolation from any human contact. The theme of seclusion is also incorporated through the repetition of the adjective "little" (ll. 2-4) to describe herself, her world, and the home she dreams up for herself and herself only. In the same way, as a child I found myself constructing an imaginary land that consisted of my favorite novel settings. The concept of building a home in my mind that was everything I could want would lead me to delve deeper into my mind, shutting out reality and everyone in it. In line five, she sings "fed my house guests bark and leaves" as a part of her playing "pretend." She feeds her guests inedible substances, revealing that they do not need actual nutrients to be sustained. Since her invisible friends exist only in her mind, and they are not in fact living, the girl can only give of herself without receiving anything in return. This concept correlates with my own puerile mentality as I would treat the characters I "met" in my books as my companions. My rationale in doing so was that our lunchtime "conversation" trumped one that I could be having with my vital friends. After describing her youth, the artist continues on to explain that she had a dream that she "could fly / from the highest swing" (ll. 8-9). The fact that she is able to soar from the tallest of swings indicates a sense of invincibility. Likewise, as long as I remained in the illusive realm, I could not be physically harmed, and if I disliked what I read I could simply close the book. From my naïve blue eyes, I believed that

I could be completely satisfied in something entirely intangible, but I would soon find the truth to be the contrary.

In theory, there was nothing wrong with my love of the fictional world, but in reality, I loved the curiosities of these characters more than my own. It was not that I was some pitiful outcast, but my life was nothing out of the ordinary. Little did I know, that was all about to change. Simarily, in lines eleven and twelve of *Dream,* Ahn reflects on "long walks in the dark / through the woods grown behind the park"(ll.11-12). All of a sudden, the mood of the song takes a more serious, almost ominous, tone. The "long walks" (l. 11) through the "woods" (l.12) symbolize a strenuous, drawn out journey through a place or time filled with fearful uncertainty. In contrast, the following lines depict an image of "stars" (l.14) smiling "down at" (l.14) her, as an illuminating guide through the darkness. I entered my dark forest when I came to the realization that real life was no longer playful or even prosaic, but rather it had become a trying struggle. In middle school and the beginning of high school, my family was a broken, chaotic mess. From the outside, we appeared to have it all together. We were a well-off Christian family, but behind the façade was a group of divided people who were constantly consumed by the attitude of a workaholic and alcoholic father. In the midst of my pain, I turned to God for answers. The artist speaks of her asking God who she is "supposed to be"(l. 13) and that He "answered in silent reverie"(l. 15). The word choice "reverie" parallels the motif of dreams because rather than God directly speaking to her, He shows her through the familiar dreamlike state that she has been enthralled with all along. Through my faith, I did not receive plainly dictated directions that I should take. Instead, my path of stars consisted of uncovering my purpose in life through the gifts I had been blessed with and the desires that were laid upon my heart.

Today, I can say that my days are no longer dominated by routine. If I want to get in my car and drive two hours to drink in the beauty of a waterfall, I will. Instead of keeping my music a secret, I play at local coffee shops for the sake of possibly being heard. After growing up in California, I find myself in the unfamiliar state of Georgia. Why, you may ask? Because it is an entirely new playground for me to conquer. I never want to get stuck in a rut of complacency and comfort. In the second chorus, the singer once again mentions her dream where she "could fly" (l. 18), but instead of a swing, her launching pad is "the highest tree" (l.19). This time, her starting point is not associated with childhood leisure, but rather thriving growth that is an even greater leap than her initial flight. I am at that same point in my own personal journey. Boundaries and fears do not hold me back. The beauty of releasing anxiety has become crucial in my walk with the Lord and living in the present tense. I am here, right at this moment, and that is exactly where I want to be.

With that said, I am quite the hypocrite. While I have realized the fragility of life and the importance of embracing a spontaneous lifestyle, my passion still remains in the imaginary realm. As I enter these next four years in hopes of expanding my knowledge, I have my future ambition in mind. In the song's final stanza, the woman concludes with describing her condition at the end of her life: "I lived it full, I lived it well / As many tales I lived to tell" (ll. 24-25). Her life experiences have become anecdotes that she has passed on to others. One day I will be writing screenplays or novels for other beings to get lost in, but instead of living through my creation, I will inspire my characters through my personal adventures.

Word Count: 1403

Dream by Priscilla Ahn Lyrics

- I was a little girl
- Alone in my little world
- Who dreamed of a little home for me
- I played pretend between the trees
- And fed my house guests bark and leaves
- And laughed in my pretty bed of green

- I had a dream
- That I could fly
- From the highest swing
- I had a dream

- Long walks in the dark
- Through woods grown behind the park
- I asked God who I'm supposed to be
- The stars smiled down at me
- God answered in silent reverie
- I said a prayer and fell asleep

- I had a dream
- That I could fly
- From the highest tree
- I had a dream

- Now I'm old and feeling gray
- I don't know what's left to say
- About this life I'm willing to leave
- I lived it full, I lived it well
- As many tales I lived to tell
- I'm ready now, I'm ready now
- I'm ready now
- To fly from the highest wing
- I had a dream

Taylor Stark

Ms. Young

English 1102

23 November 2010

The Sound of Acceptance

"But if a man does know he's about to die and dies anyway. Dies–dies willingly, knowing that he could stop it, then–I mean, isn't that the type of man who you want to keep alive?" In the film, *Stranger than Fiction*, author Karen Eiffel poses this question concerning Harold Crick, the main character in her new novel. Harold is an auditor for the Internal Revenue Service, he lives alone, he is extremely gifted in mathematical calculations, and his life is being narrated by a female, British voice. Initially, the protagonist is a timid man dominated by a formulaic ordinary life, but as he is faced with the possibility of death, his character completely evolves. Many scenes incorporate musical pieces that accent the action and dialogue on screen, while forwarding the plot on their own. The varying instrumentation and song styles presented in this film walk hand in hand with Harold's character development from security to freedom to sacrifice.

The first scene of the film begins with a shot of the world from outer space. As the camera zooms in, chaotic clock ticking and watch alarm sounds are present behind a narrator's voice introducing Harold. The shot concludes with his wristwatch beside him on his nightstand. Those sounds along with the emphasis of his wristwatch are the first indications that time is a crucial element in the plot. As Harold begins his habitual routine, the voice describes the intricate details involved, and a piano is introduced. This piano intros into an instrumental section of the song *The Way We Get By* by Spoon. Throughout the song, the piano beat is stiff, and it is accented by a tambourine, drums, and hand claps that mimic that same fast-paced even tempo. The methodical rhythm of the song adds to the preciseness of Harold's daily schedule. On top of the instrumentation, the song's title allows the audience to infer that Harold is just "getting by" with each day. The absence of lyrics highlights the narrator's voice as she gives insight into Harold's actions and the motives behind them. The music in *Stranger than Fiction*'s opening scene characterizes the main character as a man dominated by the repeated pattern he has abided by every day of his life.

After Harold hears of his "imminent death," he begins to release himself from his typical cycle and he embraces his underlying ambitions. When professor Hilbert asks him if he has any aspirations, Harold responds by explaining that he has always wanted to learn to play the guitar. From there, he buys a guitar and pursues his goal with full force. Later on, he realizes he must take initiative with his feelings toward the baker he is auditing, Ana Pascal, so he brings her baking flours as a peace offering. After they enjoy dinner together, Ana is in the kitchen washing dishes, and Harold picks up her guitar and sits down to play. Each strum is filled with devotion, and he sings quietly with his eyes closed. Ana watches him from a distance and as he continues, she is enthralled with the melody. She mouths the words of the song and then sinks into the couch beside him, looking at him longingly. When he opens his eyes, she kisses him passionately and the guitar falls to the side. Right then the recording of the song he was playing, *Whole Wide World* by Wreckless Eric, kicks in. The contrast from the timid acoustic performance by Harold and the upbeat, electric rock recording, demonstrates the distinct before and after. When he begins to play, he is courageously professing his love for Ana, despite his fears. He sings the prominent line in this song's chorus: "I'd go the whole wide world / Just to find her" (ll. 6-7). This lyric demonstrates the uncomfortable strides Harold had to take in order to portray his feelings for Ana. When the song transitions to the recording, that hard rock sound reflects Ana's reception of Harold's love.

The division of *Whole Wide World* marks the point of the story when Harold opens himself up to love, which is something he never seemed to give much thought to before he met Miss Pascal.

"Penny, I killed them all," exclaims Karen Eiffel as she realizes that Harold is one of many characters she sentenced to death. As she stares at the ceiling reflectively, the beautiful piano piece, *Horizon Variations* by Max Richter, fades in, and the scene changes to focus on Harold reading the novel on a bus. The score differs from the first scene's music in that the piano is no longer staccato, but rather, it flows smoothly and effortlessly. Also, the song is not accompanied by any percussion instruments to enforce a steady rhythm. The transformation of the piano playing style from the first scene to this one towards the end of the film follows the protagonist's metamorphosis. Harold leaps off the bus to catch Ms. Eiffel, with the novel in hand and a slight grin on his face. While she seems flustered, Harold remains confident and calm as he explains that the book is incredible. Harold continues to say, "There is only one way it can end...I love your book, and I think you should finish it." The song is an anthem of Harold's acceptance of his looming death. The melodic and self-assured piano playing style reveals a maturity that Harold has now reached. He no longer faces his death with fear, but with a selflessness that could only sprout from a life well lived. In only a short time, this man went from a monotonous life to one of spontaneity and love. The realization he comes to that the quality of life trumps the quantity enables Harold to become a noble martyr.

In *Stranger than Fiction*, the protagonist's lifestyle alteration is defined not only by his words and actions, but also the musical accompaniments that are introduced alongside the plot. The songs illustrate Harold's transformation from a man of fearful comfort into a courageous hero. At first, Harold is characterized by the short predictable piano notes played in *The Way We Get By.* When he hears of his death, he decides to take his life, as well as the soundtrack of the film, into his own hand by professing his love to Ana through song. When given the chance to escape his written fate, Harold refuses because he understands what matters most in his own life and life as a whole. The piano reappears, but this time in a completely different fashion, just as Harold has become an entirely different man. In this case, the musical accompaniments speak the greatest truth about Harold Crick.

Word Count: 1123

Works Cited

Stranger Than Fiction. Marc Forster. Dir. Columbia Pictures. 2006. Film. Lyrics: *Whole Wide World* by Wreckless Eric.

Taylor Stark

Revision Exhibit

This paragraph is an excerpt from my first Paper in the class that focused on integrating personal experiences and song analysis. On hearing the prompt for the paper, I was intrigued and excited to put my thoughts to paper. However, I began to realize that I could easily give personal accounts and analyze a song, but I had no earthly idea how to combine the two. This revision exhibit displays the evolution from a choppy paragraph full of ideas to one with smooth, complementary analysis. This first draft contains spelling errors and lacks transitions; there is a noticeable imbalance between my story and analysis of the song. After receiving feedback from my classmates and professor as well as rereading the paper myself, I believe I was able to construct a more cohesive and in-depth paragraph.

In theory, there was nothing wrong with my love of the fictional world, but in reality, I loved the curiosities of these characters more than my own. It was not that I was some pitiful outcast, but my life was nothing out of the ordinary. In lines eleven and twelve, the persona speaks of "long walks in the dark / through the woods grown behind the park." All of a sudden, the mood of the song takes a more serious, almost ominous, tone. The most distinct aspect of growing up occurred when I came to the realization that real life was no longer playful or even prosaic, but rather it had become a trying struggle. In middle school and the beginning of highschool my family was a broken, chaotic mess. From the outside, we appeared to have it all together. We were a well-off Christian family, but behind the façade was a group of divided people who were constantly consumed by the attitude of a workaholic and alcoholic father. In the midst of my pain, I turned to God for answers. The artist speakes of her asking God who she is "supposed to be"(l. 13) and that He "answered in silent reverie"(l. 15) Through my faith, I did not receive plain spoken directions or a map that illustrated the paths I should take. Instead, I began to uncover my purpose in life through the gifts I had been blessed with and the desires that were laid upon my heart.

In my second draft, I concentrated on adding more evidence to enhance the parallel of the song to my life story. Also, I corrected a spelling error and restructured sentences to get my point across more directly.

Second Draft:

In theory, there was nothing wrong with my love of the fictional world, but in reality, I loved the curiosities of these characters more than my own. It was not that I was some pitiful outcast, but my life was nothing out of the ordinary. Little did I know, that was all about to change. Similarly, in lines eleven and twelve of *Dream,* Ahn reflects on "long walks in the dark / through the woods grown behind the park." All of a sudden, the mood of the song takes a more serious, almost ominous, tone. In contrast, the following lines depict an image of "stars" (l.14) smiling "down at" (l.14) her, as an illuminating guide through the darkness. The most distinct aspect of growing up occurred when I came to the realization that real life was no longer playful or even prosaic, but rather it had become a trying struggle. In middle school and the beginning of high school my family was a broken, chaotic mess. From the outside, we appeared to have it all together. We were a well-off Christian family, but behind the façade was a group of divided people who were constantly consumed by the attitude of a workaholic and alcoholic father. In the midst of my pain, I turned to God for answers. The artist speaks of her asking God who she is "supposed to be" (l. 13) and that He "answered in silent reverie" (l. 15). The word choice "reverie" parallels with the motif of dreams because rather than God directly speaking to her, He shows her through the familiar dreamlike state that

Comment: I added a sentence as well as "Similarly" to have a smooth transition into song analysis.

Comment: Here I introduced the lines following as a way for reader to understand the full picture that would reflect my personal life.

Comment: Spelling error: Split 'highschool' into two separate words.

Comment: Spelling error: I changed "speakes" to "speaks"

she has been enthralled with all along. ¦Through my
faith, I did not receive plainly dictated directions that
I should take.¦Instead, my path of stars consisted of
uncovering my purpose in life through the gifts I had
been blessed with and the desires that were laid upon
my heart.

> **Comment:** I added analysis of the lines I quote instead of assuming the reader understands my thought process.

> **Comment:** I made this sentence brief and to the point.

**In my third draft, I focused on inserting
deeper song analysis of the lines I included in my
paragraph to strengthen my argument. Also, I
reworded a sentence in order to properly compare
the song and my own experience. After making
these final adjustments, I feel as if the paragraph
incorporates evidence, coherent analysis, and clear
correlations that contribute to my paper's thesis.**

Third Draft:

In theory, there was nothing wrong with my
love of the fictional world, but in reality, I loved the
curiosities of these characters more than my own. It
was not that I was some pitiful outcast, but my life
was nothing out of the ordinary. Little did I know,
that was all about to change. Similarly, in lines eleven
and twelve of *Dream,* Ahn reflects on "long walks
in the dark / through the woods grown behind the
park"(ll.11-12). All of a sudden, the mood of the
song takes a more serious, almost ominous, tone.
The "long walks" (l. 11) through the "woods" (l.12)
symbolize a strenuous, drawn out journey through
a place or time filled with fearful uncertainty. ¦In
contrast, the following lines depict an image of "stars"
(l.14) smiling "down at" (l.14) her, as an illuminating
guide through the darkness. I entered my dark forrest
when I came to the realization that real life was

> **Comment:** Rather than just stating that the tone changes, I explain what in the song leads me to believe that.

no longer playful or even prosaic, but rather it had become a trying struggle. In middle school and the beginning of high school my family was a broken, chaotic mess. From the outside, we appeared to have it all together. We were a well-off Christian family, but behind the façade was a group of divided people who were constantly consumed by the attitude of a workaholic and alcoholic father. In the midst of my pain, I turned to God for answers. The artist speaks of her asking God who she is "supposed to be"(l. 13) and that He "answered in silent reverie"(l. 15). The word choice "reverie" parallels with the motif of dreams because rather than God directly speaking to her, He shows her through the familiar dreamlike state that she has been enthralled with all along. Through my faith, I did not receive plainly dictated directions that I should take. Instead, my path of stars consisted of uncovering my purpose in life through the gifts I had been blessed with and the desires that were laid upon my heart.

Comment: I reworded this sentence so that it would tie into the previous thought mentioned about the song.

Taylor Stark

Peer Review Exhibit

During my high school years, I never allowed anyone to proofread my paper before I turned it in. In reality, I would usually sit down at my computer and just write until I could no longer formulate coherent thoughts. Then I would glance over my paper for grammatical errors and then I would turn in that paper as my final. I never saw anything wrong with my so-called process because my writing was typically well-received, but I did not realize I was not reaching my full potential.

This year I have not only learned the value of having my work peer edited, but also that in reading my fellow students' writing. After sitting in front of a paper for hours, I tend to lose focus in my paper's argument. With a fresh pair of eyes looking over my words, my classmates were able to shed light on technical mistakes as well as give insight concerning my analysis. In the same way, as I peer review other students' essays, I am able to mirror those corrections in my own work. Oftentimes I have seen an issue in someone else's paper and realize that I have made the same error in my own work. The process of peer review has enriched my ability to fine tune and assess my own writing through means of comparison.

Music's Bittersweet Effect on my Life by Kendall Griffy

It was a creative outlet that allowed me to lose myself in my music and let go of my worries. It allowed me

> **Comment**: I don't know if it matters, but since you are starting a new paragraph you might want to introduce the oboe again instead of starting the sentence with "it".

to focus my energy on something productive, and I was able to interpret the work of others and translate my own emotions through the notes of others. The music was angry, lighthearted, and passionate. It put into motion all of the emotions that welled inside. Not only did music ease my anxiety, it brought me closer to my father. My dad's passion for music gave us a common bond, and there was an unspoken appreciation for it that made us so close. We would drive to rehearsals together, and we'd go and see live performances. My family could enjoy something as a whole.

> **Comment:** Really like this idea of translating your emotions through the notes of other. Maybe phrase it differently though since in the same sentence you said "of others" twice.

> **Comment**: I think you could end this paragraph with something more profound. You describe it with such detail, but then this last sentence is kind of short and surfacy.

A *Bit of Strawberry in the Recording* by Blake Turner

While "Strawberry Fields Forever" may have changed the world it started out just like any other recording. While in Spain during the filming of a Spanish film, John Lennon the front man of the band began work on what would become "Strawberry Fields Forever". Lennon began by reminiscing about his childhood in which there was a place he used to frequent called Strawberry Field. Strawberry Field was actually a Salvation Army Children's Home near where Lennon grew up. As Lennon began mapping out the song he came to identify Strawberry Field as a place of comfort and safety. After finding his hook for the song Lennon began psycho analyzing himself which is apparent in the lyrics, "No one I think is in my tree," "There's no one on my wavelength,"(Strawberry Fields) all of these comments show how a depressed

> **Comment**: Insert comma

> **Comment**: I would rephrase this the "Spanish film" seems redundant. Maybe say, "While on set for a film in Spain, ..." or something along those lines.

> **Comment**: Citing should just have line numbers

> **Comment**: I would put a period and begin a new sentence here.

Lennon felt that no one understood him. Many believe these lyrics came to fruition due to Lennon's failing marriage with then wife Cynthia Powell and the tail end of a terrible previous tour (500 Greatest Songs). As the song progressed from a simple idea of safety and nostalgia so did Lennon's psychoanalysis of himself. Instead of feeling like the lone man Lennon began to embrace the idea of his individuality and obscurity with lyrics such as, "they can't hang you for it," and "I mean it's not too bad,"(Strawberry Fields) all of which strengthened Lennon's attempt for self-acceptance. While Lennon's original acoustic version contained no refrain when he eventually brought it in to the studio – the song and the recording world would be changed for future generations.

The "Ice Dance" Theme and it's Importance in Edward Scissorhands by Kendall Griffy

In the "Ice Dance" theme's first occurrence, Kim opens the door to find Edward carving an angel into ice. Following a quick flourish in the string section, the music crescendos. The gentle "ooh" sounds of a boys choir dip in and out of the string melody resulting in a magical melody that fits the mood of the scene . Edward has reached a point of enlightenment in the form of feeling love for someone for the first time. For this reason, the theme becomes the closest thing to a love song in the movie. A variation of it is played whenever feelings arise between Edward and

> **Comment:** Last mention on the source, I promise. It should say the authors name then the page number. It's the same for all of the outside sources except the song, which I already wrote above.

> **Comment:** It would be helpful to have a little background of this character

> **Comment:** I love your description of the instrumentation and music.

Kim. In attempt to show his love for Kim, he carves her an angel which she begins to dance around. At this point it begins to snow in suburbia for the first time so the audience begins to associate the theme with snow and winter. This is the reason the theme is called the "Ice Dance." The other-worldly sounding boys choir most fittingly represents Edward musically. The choir sounds eerie, not unlike Edward's appearance, but is unmistakably beautiful to the ear. When the scene changes, the audience is left on sustained note that is the not the tonic. This creates a feeling of incompleteness, much like a cliffhanger ending in a movie. Elfman uses this technique strategically. We must wait until the very end of the film, during the scene titled "The End," to hear the melody finally draw to a close.

The Ice Dance theme reappears in the last scene where a much older Kim is telling a bedtime story to a young girl. The story is of Edward Scissorhands. The familiar musical theme fades in from silence. We hear the tinkering bells of the celeste, the gentle oohs from the boys choir, and the string section in it's entirety as snow begins to fall outside the window. When the camera pans out so the audience sees Edward's gothic castle on the hill, the young girl asks if Edward is still alive. When Kim rationalizes that he must be because before Edward came around, there was no snow, the tide changes. Now the little girl and the audience has reached a point of enlight-

Comment: This sentence is a bit awkward. I would say something like, "Paralleling, the musical piece derives its name from this prominent wintery setting."

Comment: Don't say "not unlike" because it is a double negative. Rather just say that the choir reflects the physical appearance of Edward.

Comment: Take "the" out. (I think that is how you intended the sentence to read)

Comment: This phrase seems to just be tagged on at the end, creating a run on feel. Try and reword this sentence to make it a smooth transition into your next thought.

enment. We know that Edward, although fleeing Suburbia, is still alive and in love with Kim. `‗ _ _ _ _ _ ‗

I feel that these three examples of my peer reviews display distinct aspects of my editing abilities and approach.

Comment: I think you can go more in depth in this paragraph. Explain further the importance of the same piece appearing in a completely different situation. Also there is not much about the music. Even though you already explained it's composition earlier in the paper, you can still illustrate its emphasis.

Taylor Stark

Wild Card - Poem

I initially wrote this poem as a supplement to my first essay titled "Fabrication to Freedom." The poem discusses my transformation from a child consumed in the imaginary relm, to a young adult in search of adventure. I chose this poem as my Wild Card exhibit because it depicts the structure and writing style that I love. It is a free verse poem that incorporates some poetic devices, but there is not much of a consistent pattern throughout the piece. With this assignment I did not feel any pressure to conform my writing, but rather I was able to lay it out exactly how I desired. The poem "Fictional Life" reflects my unrestrained lifestyle and writing.

Fictional Life

It was all in my dreams
Pages held my world into place
Words were my means of transportation
Setting was my place of habitation and residence
Plot was my everyday life without tangible consequence
Characters were mere reflections of my desired self

Defined by the adventures of fabricated men and women
I lived the quiet and vicarious life

I explored all corners of the earth
I interacted with the most fascinating creatures
I felt the deepest heartbreaks and the most passionate love
What could I say for myself?
What could I call my own?

Defined by the adventures of fabricated men and women
I lived the quiet and vicarious life

My body would lie in a box six feet under
My headstone would read only of my birth and death
My existence would be as dust in the wind
I wanted something more
I needed something more

No longer to be defined by the adventures of fabricated men and women
I embarked on a journey labeled with my name

I touch the trees and feel the earth between my worn toes
I am not invincible, my flesh is vulnerable and mortal
I feel despair and great joy; envy no longer flows through my veins
What can I conquer next?
What is my next step?

When my body is feeble and worn down
When I can no longer skip or see the cracks in the pavement
I will dig back into my content memory and recall
I will relive the days of my youth and put pen to paper
For there is at least one child waiting to dream

Courtney Purvis's Portfolio

🌐 That Deceit Should Dwell in Such a Gorgeous Palace	Biography Download
🌐 A Method to the Madness	Introductory Reflective Essay Download
🌐 My Dull Brain Was Wrought With Things Forgotten	Exhibit of Revision Process Download
🌐 The Fortunate Unhappy: A Potential Remedy	Revised Essay 1 Download
🌐 Fiend Angelical: The Honorable Villian, Atrazine	Revised Essay 2 Download
🌐 Oh! Happy Dagger! Cut Thy Page!	Exhibit of Peer Review Process Download
🌐 Parting is Such Sweet Sorrow	Wild Card Download

ENGL1102

Student: Courtney Purvis

Teacher: Sharon McCoy

Courtney Purvis's ePortfolio is memorable for its lively range of styles, from the lyrical (in her Biography) to the hard-core scientific (in "Fiend Angelical"). It is also notable for its ability to convey through these various styles the author's equally strong commitment to both science and art. The topics of Courtney's essays may strike some readers as unusual; she was a member of the Fall 2010 Life Sciences Learning Community, a class composed of both English 1101 and 1102 students that was oriented to the scientific kinds of topics the students encountered in Chemistry and in the Learning Community's First-year Seminar. Courtney's instructor writes: "Don't be fooled by the smooth and unforced structure of her essays or her portfolio: these were the product of much frustration, passion, and determination to find the keys that hold it all together beautifully."

Writer's ethos: From the Biography's image to the concluding poem, Courtney's portfolio gives a vivid portrait of its author. To some extent, we "know" the writer through *what* she says. Courtney is particularly good at explaining her creative process. Her Introductory Reflective Essay, for instance, describes the writing of a paragraph as a documentary: "The scene opens and a narrator introduces the topic at hand with a weighted and urgent tone. The voice (which normally sounds like Edward Norton) uncovers the research while interrogating the watcher about their knowledge of the case with deep, thought-provoking extremes." At other times, we sense the writer's ethos by *how* she says things – through style.

Unity: As in the case of Brittany Scott, Courtney gives unity to her ePortfolio through thematic titles that link her essays together. In this case, the titles use thematically appropriate Shakespearean quotations, helping to reinforce the juxtaposition of art and science in Courtney's work. The poem included as the Wild Card itself plays with Shakespearean diction. The Introductory Reflective Essay also helps to unify the portfolio by establishing connections between its parts. The two revised essays, for instance, "are pieces about a helpful hormone, oxytocin, and a possibly harmful herbicide, atrazine"; parallel sentence structure and alliteration underscore economically the relationship between the two pieces.

Style: Courtney's own prose style contributes importantly to her ethos. She switches frequently from a scientific to a conversational voice in a way that helps her argument rather than simply disrupt the essay's unity. A good example can be found in "The Fortunate Unhappy," where the author begins with a hypothetical anecdote—"Imagine being in a room surrounded by empty faces of characters speaking with monotonous voices"—to give the reader a sense of what it feels like to be schizophrenic; but by the third paragraph she recounts in a straightforward manner a scientific experiment.

Biography

"Oh! that deceit should dwell in such a gorgeous palace!"

I sit with ivories in hand at all times, in all places. There is always a tune caught in my ears or a note stuck on my tongue and then I'm off, with fingers flickering at my sides. I am a pianist not by schooling, but by definition. What I hear and what I feel becomes what I play. My temperament is more likely to cause a shift in the buoyancy of my hands and the sound they produce more than any tiny Italian sign scribbled at the top of a page. Inspiration comes to me from the beauty of simple things and the oddities of others. My joy is finding the balance between them and then trying to convey that in music; forte and piano, staccato and legato, the sleek black and classy white keys. The music that catches my ear involves juxtaposing elements, a kind of "organized chaos."

I am the music I play.

The juxtaposing elements I adore in music are traits I often find within myself. I don't like groups of large, boisterous people, but I absolutely love being in a choir. Nothing excites me more than playing in front of an audience and getting feedback, but at the same time I am far too timid to speak in front of a crowd. Moreover, I am half deaf and losing my hearing, yet I prefer to play piano by ear (well, the right one, anyway). I sit back and listen to a part a few times, close my eyes, flex my hands over the keys, and stumble between black and white until I find that sweet chord that captures the previous melody. It's art at its clumsiest, and I'm addicted.

I am the music I read.

At first appearance you see a peaceful, uniform page, but after delving into the notes you may find something unexpected; a wild chord of dissonance or sudden resolve. You may see a pretty face held by a delicate, slender frame. While on the outside I appear calm and collected, I assure you I am a bit of a basket-case. I am both sarcastic and frank, spontaneous and reserved, gregarious and introverted, with the mornings and the evenings.

I am light and dark like the keys that tremble at my whim.

You see a piano, but you can't see the music it's capable of.

Introductory Reflective Essay

"A Method to the Madness"

Courtney Purvis

I find it easiest to express myself through poetry or song, which is quite difficult to carry into a class with a focus in scientific studies. Nevertheless, scientific research can begin with a poetic start and be molded into something more evidence-based and straightforward. This process is slightly problematic, for if the science and style aren't combined properly, a piece will crumble like organized chaos. I've tried to discover a method to the madness of my poetic writing style, but I fear that analyzing my thought processes will only damn the dam of poetic flow and lead me to drown you with accidental alliteration arriving with metaphor and personification alongside. If that is, however, the most effective way of explaining my method, then allow me to return to my initial style. Writing is like rearing a child. Birth is often viewed as the most painful task, but the true difficulty comes with growth: shaping the child and raising it to succeed in society. I admit I struggle with initially shaping a paper, but the more Herculean load is to change what my mind has already dedicated to the page. I had to learn that a perfect first draft is hard to come by, as a first attempt at writing does not fully develop a complete command of the logic or efficacy that the writer is capable of. You must learn to walk before you can run. As a writer, you must plan before you write and fail before you ever write well.

As a writer who begins scientific research with a chorus of hypothetical situations, I am not a stranger to preliminary failure. The most beneficial tool in discovering the mistakes of preliminary writing is peer review. Another editor with a different perspective will force the writer to see the mistakes he looks over. Humans are proud creatures; acknowledging and correcting our faults takes dedication and courage. It is the same with writing. The hardest part of composition is cutting our attachments to the original seed from our mind and allowing something else to replace it. Therefore, as most of my papers are written in poetic styling, a lot must be sacrificed and polished for clarity. If not, my paper would look more like a plan for research to come rather than an analysis of several studies, like several of my research projects this year first appeared. So I don't lose track of my purpose in writing, I must constantly remind myself that my audience would much rather read the data and conclusions I provide them than to be lead through a hypothetical questionnaire about the deeper meaning of the topic. However, I do often fall back into my own style of my writing.

To elaborate, a paragraph usually emerges from my mind as a documentary rather than a paper. The scene opens and a narrator introduces the topic at hand with a weighted and urgent tone. The voice (which normally sounds like Edward Norton) uncovers the research while interrogating the watcher about their knowledge of the case with deep, thought-provoking extremes. A montage of serious men and women in lab coats discuss their current findings and then the audience is left to decide who is in the wrong or if their science is relevant at all to the world. The scene works wonderfully, but only as a vision of what I want the readers to see. My job after that is to explore the scene and fill in the blanks with evidence-based reading. It is my hope that this practice will create a dialogue between my paper and the audience to enhance understanding. My intention in writing is not just to get the reader to understand my research, but to see the importance of timely work and the pertinence of the issue in society by feeling like they've delved into the research themselves.

The task of combining poetry with science is not an easy one. At times it seems as if they are complete opposites. The success of my writing will only come with balancing these two loves, so I have dedicated my portfolio to a man who was able to master opposing elements, William Shakespeare. Each piece is titled with one of Shakespeare's many oxymora that play on the theme or content of the work. My two essays are pieces about a helpful hormone, oxytocin, and a possibly harmful herbicide, atrazine. They both deal with research whose outcome will greatly affect the lives of many. Oxytocin is a hormone many doctors use in labor, but may also prove to be an aid for the mentally ill. Titled from a line from *Twelfth Night*, "The Fortunate Unhappy: A Remedy for Schizophrenia," the article explains a possibility for improving the lives of socially handicapped schizophrenics. On the other hand, "Fiend Angelical: The Debate of the Honorable Villain, Atrazine," named for Shakespeare's *Romeo and Juliet* (Shakespeare's Oxymora), explains a commonly found herbicide that is putting the nation at risk. In both pieces, I struggled greatly to capture the significance of the research and the possible impact it could have on the world. The importance would not have been conveyed without meticulous editing.

To demonstrate the detailed process of revision, I have included an excerpt from "The Fortunate Unhappy," where I initially denied my poetic style and wrote a horribly mediocre introduction. With excessive nit-picking, I molded the paragraph to a form which is far more appealing to read and introduces the issue by grabbing your attention instead of causing you to grab your pillow. The only line that truly describes my frustration at ignoring my original method is a line from *Macbeth,* where the king states, "My dull brain was wrought with things forgotten" (Shakespeare's Oxymora). The excerpt precedes the final draft of the essay to assure an easy comparison of the two. Another essential component to writing is peer revision. After editing your own essay, it is greatly beneficial if a peer looks it over to find problems with flow or explanation. My peer review of a classmate's work named "Oh! Happy Dagger! Cut Thy Page!" is another allusion to *Romeo and Juliet* (Shakespeare's Oxymora). In this peer annotation, I point out conflicts that will allow the writer to deftly condense his work and better his clarity. Peer critiques have allowed my papers to reach a dialogue between writer and reader that I never thought capable of my own hand. If any paper proves successful, it will be because failures were recognized in the primary drafts and corrected.

Finally, my last piece, "Parting is Such Sweet Sorrow," is a dedication in remembrance of a woman who acted as my adoptive mother when my mother became gravely ill in my childhood. I originally wrote it as a limerick to alleviate the stress at her passing, but rewrote it as a sonnet because she deserves something more beautiful. It is the method to my madness in the simplest way I know how to describe: a poem.

My portfolio itself is a dedication to the select few who adore the eclectic blend of science and poetry.

Works Cited:

"Shakespeare's Oxymora." *Squidoo*. Web. 27 Nov. 2010. <http://www.squidoo.com/shakespeare-oxymorons>.

"My Dull Brain Was Wrought With Things Forgotten"

A Self Revision

Courtney Purvis

Writers Note: The two paragraphs are an excerpt from the paper, "'The Fortunate Unhappy:' A Remedy for Schizophrenia." This is the first draft for the introduction to the research on oxytocin and Schizophrenia.

Draft 1:

The population consisting of people with crippling mental disorders is ever increasing. Those suffering from schizophrenia are able to discern their own emotions, but can not discern those of others. Oxytocin, a neuropeptide, could be the solution, but the full relation between schizophrenia and the hormone is unknown. Given current research, oxytocin could be used to treat largely overlooked symptoms of schizophrenia.

Schizophrenia is classified as a mental disorder that affects social behaviors and thought process. It is known to cause abnormal movements and psychosis in the form of paranoia and the occurrence of extreme hallucinations. In the symptoms that are constantly overlooked are the lack of visual recognition of emotions (Resource1). People that suffer from schizophrenia often have biased opinions of themselves and others. In some cases they are conceited and sometime suffering from illusions

> **Comment:** The introduction opens with a bland statistic that doesn't focus on the topic at hand or catch the reader's attention.

> **Comment:** This is a rather confusing sentence. The parallel structure may be mistaken for repetitiveness.

> **Comment:** The solution to what? Unclear- needs more discussion.

> **Comment:** "Overlooked" seems repetitive here. Who overlooks it? Furthermore, if it is constantly overlooked than it should not be used to define the disease.

> **Comment:** Should be "delusions of grandeur."

of grandeur and elitism. In other cases they are depressed, self conscious, and have very low self-esteem (Study B).

Writer's Note: The first Introduction is somewhat mediocre. It is not very specific and things don't seem to flow from one idea to the next. The second paragraph jumps directly into a study without letting the reader see a bigger picture of things. The last few sentences of the second paragraph would be better off later in the paper and also, the citations are not correctly titled and do not include page numbers.

Final Draft:

Imagine being in a room surrounded by empty faces of characters speaking with monotonous voices. You may understand the words they say, but you are still baffled by their meaning. Unable to make a connection with anyone, you feel despondent and lost. In reality, the menagerie of unknown was just as normal as any-day interaction, just without the ability to read emotions. Schizophrenia is classified as a mental disorder that affects social behaviors and thought process. It is known to cause abnormal movements and psychosis in the form of paranoia and the occurrences of extreme hallucinations. The scenario in the room filled with ubiquitous confusion represents a symptom of schizophrenia that is constantly overlooked by the public and media; the inability to visually recognize emotions. Those

> **Comment:** This opening is much more appealing and poetic. It flows from one topic to the next very easily. The reader is immediately grabbed into the text in a unique way.

> **Comment:** These sentences are better off in text rather than introducing a study.

> **Comment:** Answers by whom it is overlooked and also ties real life to the scenario at the beginning.

suffering from schizophrenia are able to discern their own emotions, but can not discern those of others, presenting a serious impediment in social and neurological development (Dryden-Edwards 1). People with schizophrenia are not indifferent to feeling; their ability to empathize is just greatly hindered. A possible solution to this social dilemma is a neuropeptide known as Oxytocin, which is currently used to treat similar symptoms in autism (Marazziti 698). Unfortunately, the synthesized hormone has not been widely tested as a treatment for schizophrenia. Subsequently, the complete relation between schizophrenic behavior and oxytocin is yet unknown.

> **Comment:** The statement from earlier is reused, but with more evidence and discussion of its importance.

> **Comment:** Introduces oxytocin in connection to previous statements.

> **Comment:** This last sentence allows the reader to see the overall conflict that will be discussed in the paper.

Writer's Note: This final draft is much more natural in content flow. It introduces the main points of the research while supporting previous statements. The opening draws the reader's eye to the page and allows them to see through the eyes of the patient. Instead of making bland assertions, there are claims followed by data and discussion. The last few sentences of the second paragraph were removed and placed in a more suitable context. Overall, the final draft is greatly preferred to the first due to a more interesting and mature development of the subject at hand.

"The Fortunate Unhappy"
A Potential Remedy for SCHIZOPHRENIA

Courtney Purvis

Imagine being in a room surrounded by empty faces of characters speaking with monotonous voices. You may understand the words they say, but you are still baffled by their meaning. Unable to make a connection with anyone, you feel despondent and lost. In reality, the menagerie of the unknown was just as normal as any daily interaction, but without the ability to read emotions. Schizophrenia is classified as a mental disorder that affects social behaviors and thought process. It is known to cause abnormal movements and psychosis in the form of paranoia and the occurrences of extreme hallucinations. The scenario in the room filled with ubiquitous confusion represents a symptom of schizophrenia that is constantly overlooked by the public and media: the inability to visually recognize emotions. Those suffering from schizophrenia are able to discern their own emotions, but cannot discern those of others, presenting a serious impediment in social and neurological development (Dryden-Edwards 1). People with schizophrenia are not indifferent to feeling; their ability to empathize is just greatly hindered. A possible solution to this social dilemma is a neuropeptide known as oxytocin, which is currently used to treat similar symptoms in autism (Marazziti 698). Unfortunately, the synthesized hormone has not been widely tested as a treatment for schizophrenia. Subsequently, the complete relation between schizophrenic behavior and oxytocin is yet unknown.

People who suffer from schizophrenia often have biased opinions of themselves and others. In some cases they are conceited and sometimes suffer from delusions of grandeur and elitism. In other cases they are depressed, self conscious, and have very low self-esteem (Pauly et al. 1).

Understanding extreme emotions can lead to understanding the full effects of oxytocin in emotional comprehension. Recently, the Department of Psychiatry and Psychotherapy in Germany partnered with the Department of Psychology of Columbia University to conduct a study comparing these extreme self-conceptions constantly found with schizophrenia and how they affect the understanding of emotions. Fifteen patients with schizophrenia were categorized into the "positive symptoms" or "negative symptoms" regarding their self-perception. Then fifteen mentally "healthy" subjects were found and paired with a coinciding patients of similar age and background. Then all participants of the test were run through a multi-part experiment. In the first experiment, the thirty were shown a list of random adjectives of positive and negative connotation and were asked to relate the words to themselves, intimate others, or others in general. In the second procedure, a list of random personality traits are shown again with the addition of new "neutral" adjectives and the subjects were asked to perform a "lexical task" in which they would determine whom they had previously ascribed the word to, or if it was a new word altogether (Pauly et al. 5).

In encoding the results, the scientists of Colombia discovered that regardless of whether the patients were diagnosed as positively or negatively symptomatic they experienced similar test results. Schizophrenic patients underperformed the healthy subjects in the tests regarding social pictures and emotion recognition by more than 10%. However, they were surprisingly more adept at recognizing both negative and positive words they had already seen (Pauly et al. 5). It is already understood that people suffering from schizophrenia often have biased opinions of themselves, but researchers did not expect that schizophrenics would perform significantly better at the lexical task. The study proves that schizophrenia patients have similar intellectual capacity as their counterparts, even though they do not possess the ability to access emotions as easily. The emotion complex that decreases performance and memory functions in social situations is not psychological, but has a physiological origin.

The key to understanding schizophrenia lies in the physiological roots of the disease. The alteration of functions in the brain that causes schizophrenia to occur is located in the amygdala, which is known as a key component of the limbic system. This system is crucial in processing emotions and the amygdala is specifically in charge of managing emotional stimuli (Domes 1187). In another main part of the limbic system, the hypothalamus, oxytocin is produced by a large aggregation of neurons alongside another hormone known as vasopressin (Marazziti 698). Studies suggest that it could also play a significant role in managing social memory and behavior in the amygdala. A study by Zurowski B. Gamer, published in PNAS, in which oxytocin was tested regarding emotional and facial recognition suggests that oxytocin levels are "critically important for eye movements and attention" and are directly related to increasing "eye movements and attention." Where the focus of those being tested was "initially centered on the mouth" to interpret an emotion, after oxytocin was introduced, the subjects began looking at the eyes, demonstrating an understanding of the part of the face that is most significant in determining emotions (Averbeck 9034). Furthermore, oxytocin could possibly be administered to counter some of the symptoms of schizophrenia at the root of the problem (Domes 1187).

In order to determine if oxytocin could be used to alleviate some of the hardships specifically related to schizophrenia, the research of oxytocin conducted on patients without mental abnormalities must be considered. The information necessary for comparison was acquired in a double-blind study where thirteen males participated in two tests. The first test was conducted using a placebo intranasally and the second was conducted using oxytocin. Then the test subjects were shown pictures of faces depicting angry, fearful, or happy emotions while receiving an fMRI (functional magnetic resonance imaging) to capture brain activity. The patients are administered a contract dye injection that allows the MRI to monitor blood flow. If activity occurs in a specific part of the brain, expanding blood vessels will cause chemical changes by the delivery of extra oxygen, which will bring the contract dye to that area. In subjects who received the placebo, there were large amounts of activity, or percent signal changes, in the right amygdala. This means that on the fMRI, parts of the brain that changed in blood flow lit up on the scan. On the other hand, subjects that received oxytocin showed lower signal changes during the recognition of angry, fearful, and happy faces. The significant difference between activity can be related to the application of oxytocin (Domes 1189). The "lighting" of the brain during the scan indicates the work the neurons in the amygdala experience in interpreting emotional stimuli; the lighter the color of a specific part of the brain, the more processing the neurons are going through. Precise and quick decisions occur when the neurons decipher information quickly, meaning they do less work and light up for shorter amounts of time. This is true for the patients on the test where oxytocin was administered. The fMRI showed less light in those specific scans, indicating the subjects were making faster decisions (Domes 1188). If the results are uniform for all those who received oxytocin, then these results may also be true for schizophrenics.

The possibility that oxytocin is a remedy to faulty emotional interpretation is still being tested. The hormone is already being used in studies to increase social behavior and emotional recognition in autism and to assist general memory and learning (Marazziti 699). Given the significant connection that oxytocin has with schizophrenia and various other mental disorders, it could be used to reduce the harmful medications that presently treat the disease. Drugs such as olanzapine, risperidone, quetiapine, ziprasidone, and aripiprazole, which are referred to as "atypical anti-psychotics," are used to treat mental illnesses involving social disorders or psychosis. The side-effects of anti-psychotics range from tremors and early-life dementia to kidney failure and obesity (Dryden-Edwards 4). Oxytocin's secondary effects are not so severe; the most common side-effects are nausea and vomiting. Rare cases, as with all medicines, develop allergic reactions which can lead to a change in heart rate or blood clots if the medicine is still administered after reported allergy. The symptoms of oxytocin would only approach the side-effects of atypical anti-psychotics if the hormone was administered to a woman in early pregnancy, as it is frequently used to induce labor (Oxytocin Side Effects 1). Oxytocin may therefore provide a safer way to alleviate the stressful symptoms hindering the lives of schizophrenics.

Given the hormone's insignificant side-effects and the physiological symptoms of schizophrenia as shown in the Domes study, Oxytocin may be the best choice doctors have to enhance the lives of their patients. With around two million people in the United States diagnosed with schizophrenia (Dryden-Edwards 1), the need for further study of the relation between schizophrenia and oxytocin is great. Unfortunately, a substantial amount of research is needed before any hormone can be widely accepted as treatment for a neurological disease: research that has not yet been conducted with oxytocin. Scientists have already determined the possible medical implications of the hormone, but somewhere in the struggle for scientific limelight, the cause became diluted. With time and support, oxytocin could be a significant solution to the predicaments of many.

Works Cited:

Averbeck B B. Oxytocin and the salience of social cues, Proceedings of the National Academy of Sciences 2010; 107 (20): 9033-9034.

Domes G, Heinrichs M, Gläscher J, Büchel C, Braus D F, Herpertz S C. Oxytocin Attenuates Amygdala Responses to Emotional Faces Regardless of Valence, Biological Psychiatry 2007;62: 1187-1190.

Dryden-Edwards R.Schizophrenia. In: Medicine Net [discussion list on the Internet]. 2010; [cited 2010Sept. 28]. 11 p. Available from: http://www.medicinenet.com/schizophrenia/article.htm.

Marazziti D, Catena Dell'Osso M. The Role of Oxytocin in Neuropsychiatric Disorders, Current Medicinal Chemistry 2008; 15: 698-704.

"Oxytocin Side Effects." *Drugs.com*. Web. 01 Dec. 2010. <http://www.drugs.com/sfx/oxytocin-side-effects.html>.

Pauly, K., et al., Self-concept, emotion and memory performance in schizophrenia, Psychiatry Res.(2010). doi:10.1016/j. psychres.2010.08.017. 1-7.

"Fiend Angelical"
The "Honorable Villain," Atrazine
Courtney Purvis

For many years, agricultural institutions have relied on atrazine as a powerful herbicide primarily used for corn, but also on a large number of less prolific crops. It is so widely used as a pesticide that traces of atrazine have been found in over two thirds of the bodies of water in the United States (*PANNA*) due to significant runoff from irrigation. Atrazine is produced by a champion of the agribusiness industry known as Syngenta. Dr. Tyrone B. Hayes, a researcher from the University of California at Berkeley, has presented evidence that atrazine is a carcinogen in the reproductive system and a hormonally active agent due to its chemical property to interrupt the endocrine system. Hayes's research focuses primarily on atrazine's effects on amphibians, specifically hermaphroditism in frogs. However, Syngenta's head researcher, Dr. Peter Hertl, has contested Dr. Hayes's findings and questioned the validity of his research (Hertl). Despite Dr. Hertl's rejection of Dr. Hayes's research and the doubts of its scientific merit, there is significant evidence that suggests that atrazine is a dangerous endocrine disruptor and is a significant environmental hazard. While Hertl challenges Hayes's results, there is greater reason to question Hertl's motives.

Recently, the significant decline in the African frog (*Xenopus laevis)* population in southern California prompted Dr. Tyrone B. Hayes to conduct a study to clarify the effects of atrazine in the hormones and reproductive organs of maturing male frogs. He hypothesized that the rapid decline was linked to the increasing presence of atrazine in their environment. Hayes began conducting experiments by introducing atrazine in 2.5 parts per billion to forty male frogs. Out of the total raised, 90% of the testing population experienced decreased hormone levels of testosterone and decreased fertility, meaning that they are less likely to reproduce in nature. The remaining four frogs, or 10% of the testing population, did not possess nuptial pads on the lower arms, but had cloacal labia, meaning they were now effectively female. Hayes observed that the hermaphroditic frogs also had an increased amount of aromatase, the enzyme which is responsible for changing testosterone to estrogen. Of these hermaphrodites, two were mated with other atrazine-exposed males and bore offspring while the other two were dissected and examined. While surveying the frogs' anatomy, Hayes discovered that even though they were chromosomal males, after being exposed to atrazine, the frogs had been physically and chemically converted into females. In addition, all of the offspring from "atrazine-induced females" were males (Hayes, et al. 4612). If atrazine is already affecting frogs at low concentrations, because concentrations are occurring in greater numbers in the wild, it is likely that Hayes's results would prove correct for other species over time.

Hayes's most recent experiment on atrazine titled "Atrazine Induces Complete Feminization and Chemical Castration in Male African Clawed Frogs (Xenopus Laevis)," which was published in the Proceedings of the National Academy of the Sciences, is under scrutiny. Syngenta's head of Global Product Safety, Dr. Peter Hertl, wrote a letter critical of Hayes to the University of California at Berkeley and to the president of the National Academy of Sciences, stating the inadequacies of Hayes's report. Hertl made few correct accusations. First, he argues that there was no control population to compare outcomes of similar sexual growth. Yet Hayes's study includes a control group of forty male African clawed frogs (Hayes, et al. 4612). Secondly, he claims that not all the methods and procedures of the experiment were included (Hertl), which also means that Hayes did not follow the standard Good Laboratory Practices (*Nebraska Corn Kernels*). When examining Hayes's methods and results, the reader will find a complete demonstration of the experiments and a supported conclusion. Finally, Hertl claims that Hayes's experiment tested only one dosage of atrazine on frogs that were constantly handled by scientists. It is true that only one dosage of 2.5 ppb (parts per billion) of atrazine were applied to the test population, which might jeopardize the accuracy of the experiment. However, Hayes uses 2.5 ppb as the current testing environment's saturation of atrazine because it is a relatively small concentration compared to the EPA's allowed maximum concentration of 3.0 ppb. It is even possible that the actual presence in certain areas in nature could be much larger. Because the test produces such adverse effects at such a small dosage, there is concern for the possibility that more severe and human-related consequences could occur. Therefore, the test only needs one dosage to determine atrazine's potential toxicity be- cause Hayes is determining the minimal effects of atrazine. If this miniscule dosage of 2.5 ppb is enough to endanger a population of frogs, then there's no way of measuring the imminent, mass infliction atrazine can cause in larger dosages to wild populations.

While the dangers of atrazine are being debated, both men fail to mention a recurring phenomenon in frogs which could greatly alter atrazine research. It has been found that under extreme environmental pressure, various amphibians and most frogs are capable of changing sexes. Heterogamety is when two different sex chromosomes are formed in one gender. For instance, human females have two 'X' sex chromosomes while the males have an 'X' and a 'Y' chromosome, so the heterogametic sex is male. It is the heterogametic sex that is capable of disintegrating its current reproductive organs and growing functional reproductive organs of the opposite sex. In amphibians, heterogamety depends on the species, which neither Dr. Hayes nor Dr. Hertl addresses (Ogata, et al. 613). In Hayes's experiment, there are forty males in a single containment unit where members of the population are being exposed to a chemical and being handled by men with absolutely no women around. It seems as though this would be enough environmental stress to cause a male to change into a female to allow the population to survive, but because forty out of forty control frogs remained males during the testing, it shows that not even excessive handling and lab procedures will spark the transformation. Once again, Dr. Hayes's evidence stands.

While Dr. Hayes is battling Dr. Hertl's proclamations to reinstate his integrity, the company financially backing Dr. Hertl has larger things at stake. Syngenta's largest concern in regard to the situation is that atrazine was unjustly vilified by Hayes's data. Atrazine is Syngenta's highest source of revenue (Hayes). Syngenta is a mega-corporation that has millions invested in a hardy pesticide that brings loyal consumers and provides thousands of jobs. Atrazine is used in the majority of the United States and many farmers currently depend on it for the success of their crop yield ("Frogs"). Dr. Hertl's check is paid by Syngenta, while Hayes is funded by several organizations that reward education and merit such as the California Toxic Substances Research and Teaching Program, the David Foundation, and the National Science Foundation. The research that has been called into question by Syngenta was published in the Proceedings of the National Academy of the Sciences, which even the leading scientist against Hayes admitted "has a long history of publishing peer reviewed scientific papers of a high standard" (Hertl). Moreover, in 1997, Dr. Hayes was working in research for a company known as Novartis, where he discovered the possible hazards of atrazine. Instead of investigating the findings, the company restricted Hayes from spreading his research through conventions or by publishing the information. He then quit his position to research atrazine on his own terms. Hayes admits that the chemical company had greatly "hindered" his efforts to reenact the experiment (Hayes).

Three years later on November 13, 2000, Novartis joined AstraZeneca to form Syngenta (*Syngenta*). As a small company, Novartis prevented Hayes from not only finding the actual repercussions of the herbicide, but also from sharing his work with the scientific community. Now as a multi-billion dollar corporation, Syngenta is doing all in their power to keep their best product on the market.

Works Cited

"Atrazine: Syngenta's Herbicide." *Pesticide Action Network North America (PANNA)*. Web. 31 Aug. 2010. <http://www.panna.org/atrazine>.

"Company History." *Syngenta*. Web. 01 Aug. 2010. <http://www2.syngenta.com/en/about_syngenta/companyhistory.html>.

"Frogs, Atrazine and the Nutty Professor." *Nebraska Corn Kernels*. 12 Aug. 2010. Web. 23 Aug. 2010. <http://nebraskacorn.blogspot.com/2010/08/frogs-atrazine-and-nutty-professor.html>.

Hayes, Tyrone B. "Our World...Our Future." *Atrazinelovers*. Web. 23 Aug. 2010. <http://www.atrazinelovers.com/m0.html>.

Hayes, Tyrone B., V. Khoury, A. Narayan, M. Nazir, A. Park, T. Brown, L. Adame, E. Chan, D. Buchholz, T. Stueve, and S. Gallipeau. "Atrazine Induces Complete Feminization and Chemical Castration in Male African Clawed Frogs (Xenopus Laevis)." *Proceedings of the National Academmy of the Sciences (PNAS)* 10th ser. 107 (2010): 4612-617. Web.

Hertl, Peter. Letter to Dr. Ralph J. Cicerone and Dr. Randy Schekman. 1 June 2010. *Atrazine Herbicide*. Syngenta. Web. 26 Aug. 2010. <http://www.atrazine.com/Amphibians/hayes_analysis.pdf>.

Kaleita, Amy. "Environmentalist Turns to E-bullying." *Washington Times*. 11 Aug. 2010. Web. 23 Sept. 2010. <http://www.washingtontimes.com/news/2010/aug/11/environmentalist-turns-to-e-bullying/>.

Ogata, M., H. Ohtani, T. Igarashi, Y. Hasegawa, Y. Ichikawa, and I. Muira. "Change of the Heterogametic Sex From Male to Female in the Frog." *Genetics* 164 (2003): 613-20. *The Genetics Society of America*. Web. 6 Dec. 2010. <http://easybib.com/cite/form/website>.

"Oh! Happy Dagger!" Cut Thy Page!
A Peer Edit

Courtney Purvis

Writer's Note: I chose this over my other edits because Vita explained that this was one of his most helpful reviews. In the peer edit, I used more casual language so that Vita would understand my comments and at times I even added internet colloquialisms so he would be more receptive to my critiques.

Writer's Memo: Personally this essay was really hard to work with. I feel that my essay is having trouble with flow, keeping it interesting, and composition. The main purpose of this essay is to review the TMR procedure, looking at its pros, cons, and eventually finding a conclusion.

The Story of TMR (Targeted Muscle Reinnervation)

Author: Vita Cama

There comes a time in everyone's life where we think past the present, imagine incredible feats, dream impossible dreams. This time we have caught up with those dreams and become the present and the possible right before our eyes. Th human mind has created fictional stories of unimaginable creatures, the only ones close to human form were hybrids, beings known as cyborgs; one half human and the other machine- a bionic being. Only two years

Comment: I'm not exactly sure if the grammar is correct here.

Comment: This sentence is a little confusing to me. I would consider changing the word use or syntax. Do you mean that we have become present, or dreams have become present?

Comment: "Th" should be "the." Also "unimanigable" is the incorrect word here-it turns the sentence into somewhat of an oxymoron.

ago, ABC News published a report on such a being, and her name is Claudia Mitchell. The marine was in her twenties when she lost her left arm in 2004 in a tragic motorcycle accident and it wasn't until 2006, with the help of Dr. Todd Kuiken, that she became the first ever "Bionic Woman"(Black). The secret behind Claudia's transformation was Dr. Kuiken's recently developed surgery: Targeted Muscle Reinnervation (TMR).

> **Comment**: "Accident. It wasn't until 2006" would make the sentence clearer.

Dr. Todd Kuiken developed the Targeted Muscle Reinnervation procedure with the intention of completely changing the way that upper body amputees recovered and continued their lives by exchanging one crucial aspect of the original procedure: don't use non native muscles and limbs to move body parts that they weren't built for, instead use the parts that were meant for it, the nerves. In Dr. Kuiken's report, *Targeted reinnervation for enhanced prosthetic arm function in a woman with a proximal amputation: a case study*, he stated that for the conventional prostheses "existing methods of control are inadequate," that they "[allow] only a single motion to be controlled at a time; operation of the prosthetic elbow, wrist, and hand, or hook must be done sequentially"(Kuiken). For patients using a prosthesis, the control may be difficult and as such the device must be user friendly. Controlling one movement at a time extends the time of completing a task and because movements must be done in a sequential order, the patient must think more on

> **Comment**: As such is a tad confusing in this sentence.

> **Comment**: Good explanation!

their actions, thus making the movement s somewhat unnatural. "Furthermore, current methods of myoelectric control do not have a natural feel because proximal muscle functions (eg, shoulder, bicep, or triceps muscles) are not normally used to direct wrist or hand movements", thus making the prosthesis an unnatural and difficult device to use(Kuiken). The process of training someone to use a conventional prosthesis can be long and tough. The main cause of this lingering is the patient's transition from using the muscles and nerves formerly connected to their arm to using other related muscles to move body parts they were not made for. As consequence, Dr. Kuiken and those that assisted, "developed a new biological neural machine interface for individuals with amputations, called targeted reinnervation" which focuses on the transferring of the remaining functional nerves that were once connected to the amputated limb to another location(Kuiken). With this new technology, patients can now use their regular thought process to control the prosthesis and use their original body parts to control the replacement limb. The transition period of prosthesis training will not take as long and the patient's ability to control the prosthesis will increase greatly.

> Comment: I'm don't understand what myo-electric and proximal means here

The transfer of nerves is successful due to the fact that the intended area of transfer is no longer in use by the missing limb and as such the relocated nerves can and do gain control of those still functional

> Comment: Leading sentence is unclear.

muscles. The reinnervation of these muscles act as relpacement muscles for those in the lost arm. Once the nerves reinnervate the muscles, the nerves can then have muscles to flex. As the patient learns to use the muscles the number of myoelectric signals increases and so does the strength. As the patient progresses in their recovery therapy and training for prosthesis use, the patient regains feeling and control of the missing limbs nerves. Dr. Kuiken calls this incredible reconnection of use "Transfer Sensation" (Kuiken). This specific result of the Targeted Muscle Reinnervation procedure is what Todd needed for the advancement of his revolutionary motives. If patient could regain control of their arm's nerves and use their reinnervated muscles, then it is possible to restore their arm to a greater extent than the conventional prosthesis does.

> **Comment:** As in the muscles regain control? COOL

> **Comment:** I would be careful not to rely on one source entirely.

> **Comment:** If <a>patient. .ps ur topic is seriously interesting

Dr. Todd Kuiken conducted his operation on Claudia Mitchell on August, 2005. Previous to the surgery, Claudia had been trained and fitted to use "a shoulder disarticulation level prosthesis" which "consisted of a passive shoulder, a motorised elbow, a passive wrist rotator and a motorised hand"(Kuiken). This prosthesis is considered passive because it does not try to anticipate or act readily to the patient's commands. With a typical prosthesis, the user must force the prosthesis to move by flexing their shoulder or other upper body parts. This passiveness causes the user to put more stress into moving the limb and thinking in a sequential order. Before Claudia received her prosthesis, she had acquired a common phenomenom among amputees: phantom limb pain. Claudia's pain was fairly great considering that it ranked 9/10 on the Likert scale. Theories behind the pain say that the pains can be from the pain memories that the brain resends to the nerves, from the damage that the nerves received from either the surgery or accident, or from the responses from blood clots from the body trying to heal itself.

> **Comment:** A little confused what you mean here.

The doctor was given permission to operate on Claudia with her acknowledgment of the risks which "included permanent paralysis of the target muscles, recurrence of phantom limb pain, and development of painful neuromas, in addition to standard risks of elective surgery"(Kuiken). As the operation progressed, "the musculocutaneous, median, ulnar, and radial nerves were all identified by their branching pattern and cut back to normal appearing fascicles"(Kuiken). The trimming of the nerves gives the doctor an easier time moving the nerves and the patient a fresh start with nerve reconstruction and reinnervation. In efforts to increase the accessibility of the myoelectric nerve signals, "all fat and scar tissue over the remnant triceps muscle was excised to optimise the surface myoelectric signal of [the] muscle"(Kuiken). As a whole the nerves were moved from the shoulder area to the upper chest and side areas. This area was selected because the muscle sin these areas were no longer connected to the arm leaving these muscles open for reinnervation by the nerves previously attached to the arm. Two days after the operation Claudia was admitted back to her home and monitored via telephone every two weeks. The experimental procedure may cause severe side effects which may need to be attended to at the first signs. Since these are nerves being relocated, any mistakes or changes must be made quickly before the nerves reinnervate the new muscles; if those muscles are damaged because of some mistake in the TMR procedure, then finding new muscles would be a daunting task.

> **Comment:** I would try explaining the surgery in your own words. The doctor's explanations are a little anatomy intense.

> **Comment**: First signs of what exactly?

Before the operation, "functional testing was done with [Claudia's] conventional myoelectric prosthesis control" where she was required to "[move] 2 • 5-cm square blocks from one box, over a 10-cm wall, and into another box"(Kuiken). These tests measure how accurately and how well the person can control the prosthesis. This test can be used to measure progress in training, but in this study it is used to compare the ease of use between the conventional prosthesis and the experimental one. In addition to the previous test, Mitchell was also asked to perform two typical activities with her conventional prosthesis: "preparation of a peanut butter and jelly sandwich, including gathering items, preparing, cutting the sandwich in half, serving, cleaning up, and returning items to appropriate storage; and ironing a shirt, including setting up an ironing board, hanging the shirt on a hanger, safely storing the iron, and folding up the board"(Kuiken). This test is like the block and box test in the fact that they measure performance in accuracy, but the previously mentioned test measures the prostheses ability to function in real life and how well it endures regular daily life activities. Claudia Mitchell was also asked to fill a journal on her daily life with her prosthesis and record her thoughts of the prosthesis and of any changes that occurred. It is important to have the opinions and details from the patient's point of view because one this is an experimental procedure and all information should be included to develop it and second, this procedure is for all future amputees; as such, a fellow amputee should give advice and information on how to improve the procedure. Claudia was brought back to the facility on March, 2006 for training for the experimental prosthesis and for testing her reinnervated muscles. After Claudia was fitted and trained with the prosthesis she was asked to go home and repeat the process with the diary, and in about a month she returned to Dr. Kuiken for additional testing. All the testing done in this procedure because the reinnervated muscles need to be monitored for their compatability with the experimental prosthesis. There she was asked to repeat the block and box test along with the "preparation of a grilled cheese

> **Comment:** Good interpretation of the experiments effectiveness

> **Comment:** Incomplete sentence..meaning is cloudy

sandwich, including preparation in a pan on the stove using butter, cutting the sandwich in half, and serving it with a beverage, opening and closing the container, returning items to the refrigerator, and cleaning of surfaces; and preparation and serving of a tossed salad with four ingredients, including peeling and slicing, getting out items and returning them to the refrigerator, pouring dressing, covering and storing leftovers, and cleaning up"(Kuiken). This similar test was given to see the durability and the performance of both the prosthesis and the patient. Compatability, efficiency, and certainty between the prosthesis and the patient is crucial for the TMR's success. During her time there Dr. Kuiken and the other scientists conducted research on her reinnervated muscles looking for sensitivity and her ability to differentiate different sensations.

> **Comment:** I think the quotation is not needed and makes the paper longer than it needs to be. I would try explaining it in your own words in a sentence or two

The only reoccurance after the operation was Claudia's phantom limb pain, but fortunately it was treated and the surgery left no mutilation of the operated area. With no scars left, the surgery can be considered a success in appearance and in surgery performance. Three months after the surgery, Mitchell noticed the reinnervated muscles twitch when she tried to use her missing arm. A couple months later, Claudia reported that the movement had increased from twitches to contractions, which shows signs of successful reinnervation of her muscles. The movement of the new muscles indicates the progress of the reinnervated muscles and the relocated nerves. Signs of strengthening reinnervation are shown by the increase in movement, consistency, and firmness from the reinnervated muscles. At 6 months in post-operation status, Claudia's reinnervated sites were recorded by Dr. Kuiken and another, newer experimental prosthesis was made in response. The new "prosthesis had passive shoulder components. The computerised arm was programmed to use the myoelectric inputs from the TMR muscles to control the motorised hand and elbow. Two pressure-sensitive pads were mounted in the patient's socket that she used to control her motorised wrist, allowing independent, proportional, simultaneous control of all three joints" (Kuiken). In order to keep up with the results of the procedure, the scientists must be ready to adjust at any time, they have successfully done so by constructing a more advanced and compatible for the patient in a short period of time. They did such a good job that the patient actually preferred the experimental prosthesis over the conventional one.

> **Comment:** I would explain this operation more, it's purpose is hard to understand.

> **Comment:** This phrase is slightly under-developed

Claudia was then again trained and within a short amount of time she was able to do more than she could with her conventional prosthesis. In the tests performed, Mitchell's performance substantially increased to about four times faster than with her previous conventional prosthesis and in real life she was able "operate the wrist rotator with the pressure sensitive buttons at the same time as moving the hand

and elbow", but more impressive was the fact that "when she thought of opening the hand, closing the hand, bending the elbow, or straightening the elbow, the prosthesis responded accordingly"(Kuiken). The transition from the conventional prosthesis and the experimental one made such an impact on Claudia's life that she described it as "just [thinking] about moving [her] hand and elbow and they [moved]", but the most important part was her admitting that "[her] original prosthesis wasn't worth wearing—this one [was]"(Kuiken).

The results of Targeted Muscle Reinnervation have proved to be incredible: the patient was able to regain use of the nerves previously connected to their amputated limb, the phantom pains were reduced, the nerves were able to reconnect with the muscles and function well, and the prosthesis and reinnervated sites worked with great success. The future is far and bright, but just because it's far doesn't mean it's impossible. If there ever is a reminder needed, just look around and see how far we've come.

Comment: Grammar side note: as such is used multiple times and kind of threw me off while reading

Reader's Comments:

I really like the way you lead into the research topic. It leads me to believe that you have connected with your research on a personal level that allows the reader to feel more connected to the topic.

If you are worried about just reporting on the source, you might want to research the cost of the procedure and the likeliness of it being used in society. You presented the information well and I understand the majority of it, including the science, which seems very complex. The concluding paragraph is well written and summarizes the paper while adding a bright aspect to it.

Cited Sources:

Black, Nelli. "Nerve Surgery Leaves Woman With Feeling in an Arm That Isn't There." *ABC News*. ABC, 08 Sep 2008. Web. 30 Sep 2010. <file:///C:/Users/Roberto/Desktop/College/UGA%20Fall%202010/English/ABC%20News%20Bionic%20Woman.htm>.

Kuiken T A, Miller L A, Lipschutz R D, Lock B A, Stubblefield K, Marasco P D, Zhou P, Dumanian G A. Targeted reinnervation for enhanced prosthetic arm function in a woman with a proximal amputation: a case study., The Lancet 2007; 369 (9559): 371-380. Accessed 2010 Sept. 30.

"Parting is Such Sweet Sorrow"
Courtney Purvis

From barn[1] to girl I raised thee to be brave
Thy thirst quenched from the heart under my breast
Thine hope was carried by the love I gave
And now thine head from things that I bequest

I prithee my script quandaries deter
My daughter that in fact mine eyes met least
Oft times diverted our attentions were
Vouchsafe these hidden words to be released

No want of grievance laid unto thy frame
No palm be raised betwixt thy fluxive[2] eyes
For all times parted you my heart did aim
Anon a peace if in mine love abide

Glossary:

barn[1]: (n) a child
fluxive[2]: (adj) tearful; flowing

Sources:

"Shakespearean Glossary." *Kidzworld*. Web. 28 Nov. 2010. <http://www.kidzworld.com/article/3989-shakespearean-glossary>.

Crystal, David, and Ben Crystal. "A Lover's Complaint." *Shakespeare's Words*. Web. 28 Nov. 2010. <http://www.shakespeareswords.com/Poem.aspx?IdPoem=54#5894>.

Victoria Moreira's Portfolio	+ - X
🗎 Biography	Biography
⊜ IRE	Introductory Reflective Essay Download
⊜ Revised Paper 1	Revised Essay 1 Download
⊜ Revised Paper 2	Revised Essay 2 Download
⊜ Revision Exhibition	Exhibit of Revision Process Download
⊜ Peer Review Exhibition	Exhibit of Peer Review Process Download
🗎 Wildcard pdf 3_18	Wild Card

ENGL1102M

Student: Victoria Moreira

Teacher: Laura Weaver

Victoria Moreira's ePortfolio gives us a glimpse into a special kind of FYC class, one that uses Reacting to the Past pedagogy. In this class, the students engaged in a Reacting Game about Cherokee Removal from Georgia that was co-authored by her instructor. In addition to satisfying all the usual criteria for a good grade in the FYC Program, Victoria's portfolio shows distinction in virtually every one of its exhibits.

Center of Gravity: Perhaps the particular nature of this class helps Victoria's portfolio have coherence and what the FYC Grading Rubric calls a Center of

Gravity (which is similar to unity), but the portfolio also offers a particularly helpful and persuasive Introductory Reflective Essay. The IRE details clearly Victoria's intellectual journey throughout the semester and alerts readers that she has organized the ePort to chart out the changes in her perspective on Native Americans.

Evidence: If, in many ways, an ePortfolio satisfies the same criteria as an essay, then we can assess portfolio strengths through the language of the FYC Grading Rubric. One of the great strengths of Victoria's portfolio is the wealth and variety of evidence that she provides to demonstrate her learning and the breadth of critical thinking she has achieved in the course. In the first revised essay, she analyzes poems in close detail; in the second, she marshals evidence from many historical documents to construct her speech arguing against Removal. In the first essay, she adopts the cool tone of the literary critic. In the second, she speaks in the impassioned tones appropriate to her character's situation in the Reacting game. Victoria's Revision exhibit also provides strong evidence of her skill in this area by discussing in detailed, concrete terms the kinds of revisions she makes from one draft to the next. Her Peer Review Exhibit also offers a detailed and persuasive account of how she went about working with a classmate on her essay, again using the language of the Rubric to guide the portfolio's reader. Her marginal notes in this exhibit also are both copious and specific in their recommendations.

Originality: Victoria's Wild Card, her edition of the newspaper *The Phoenix*, is distinctive for its originality, as well as for its strong prose and professional document design.

I was born on August 8th, 1992. Throughout my childhood, I was a noticeably right brained child. When I began my love for music at the young age of seven, I began to cultivate my creative side. Drawing, writing, singing, playing violin and piano, and reading became the main hobbies I treasure to this day. I also enjoy spending time with my close and loud Hispanic and Italian family. The remainder of my time is either spent outside exercising and enjoying the outdoors with my friends or at the library studying. On weekends here at the University of Georgia, I enjoy spending time at my neighbor's barn. There, she boards two horses Mya and Cierra (a Native American Paintaloosa and an Appaloosa respectively). My major here at the University is biology with a minor in French, and in four years, my goal is to attend medical school and later become a neonatologist.

Victoria Moreira

Professor Weaver

English 1102M

07 December 2010

When signing up for my 1102 multicultural class with Professor Weaver, I had only a basic idea of the American Indian journey—the elementary impression that Squanto helped the Pilgrims at Plymouth Rock to survive their first winter and that many later suffered and died on the Trail of Tears. In this portfolio, you will see how my ideas and knowledge of American Indian life have developed since the beginning of the semester. Progressively throughout this portfolio, elements of their history before and after they were forced to move on reservations can be seen through each of my exhibits. I did this to share the knowledge I have gained of this culture with my audience. I specifically chose the elements of this portfolio to show how my perspectives on American Indian culture have progressively deepened.

My callow knowledge of American Indians limited my perspective on their culture. My bare frame of knowledge for these people initially came from my AP United States history class in high school. There, I learned that Native Americans, as a whole, suffered while their land was taken away by the United States and were forced to move out West. I then learned that these people were then forced onto reservations and were later provided "welfare" by the United States government. I learned the straight "facts" from a dry and biased opinion—what my history book told me was important. This impersonal approach left out much of the human perspective of the individuals involved. For example, I did not want to accept that between 2500 to 6000 Indians died on the Trail of Tears. I wanted to know about the men, women, and children—not the collective group called "Indians"— that were forced to endure this brutal trial. The pages of my text book forgot to inform me of the actual adversity that American Indian *people* endured. In this class, however, I learned about these people on an individual basis.

This course also gave me another outlook on American Indian life in the times of Indian Removal—different from what my earlier history class had taught me. In the course of the Reacting to the Past Game set in 1835 that my multicultural class played, I not only learned the history behind Cherokee removal but also the personal struggles that Cherokee people specifically endured while we settled the central issue of Indian removal. In the process of the game, three main factions were involved: the Ross faction (those opposed to removal), the Ridge Faction (those for removal), and the White Faction (those also for removal). Described in my second essay, for example, as I played the role of Elijah Hicks in class, the chief editor of the Cherokee newspaper entitled *The Phoenix*, I understood the complexity of removal among the Cherokee people. As I argued among my own friends in class of the opposing faction, I understood what it felt like to be divided even among friends on an issue that would affect an entire people. Additionally in this game, my viewpoint on Cherokee removal was further shaped by a special project I took on. I chose to end my portfolio with this project as my Wildcard because it best represented all of the varying arguments that helped shape my opinions on Removal. In the game, I was asked to put together a full-length edition of *The Phoenix.* In this edition, I was asked to collect articles from the people in both the Ross and Ridge factions, including a personal editorial that I wrote to the Cherokee people. This newspaper was a collection of viewpoints on the central question at hand on whether the Cherokee People should be forced to leave their home. In this full-length edition, I was forced, because of a vote in our game, to publish both factions' viewpoints on removal. While I tried to show that my faction was the most persuasive, the arguments from the opposing faction were also very convincing: I could see how many at the time were torn about this delicate issue. Further into the game-play as I read the primary documents that consisted of court cases, letters, editorials, and essays on the topic of removal, I began to understand the varying facets that came with the central question of removal—like the way bribes were taken by some of the Cherokee for votes among the Council and how the role of a third party White Faction had a great influence over the division between the two majorities. The game play and the literature we read shaped a significant part of my full comprehension of the individual Native American's attitude and culture.

As demonstrated in my portfolio, throughout the course of this semester I also gained a better understanding of modern American Indian culture. In my first revised essay, I compare the struggle of identity among modern American Indians as they wander between the reservation life and the new city life. In this essay, I organize my paper based on the contrasting perspectives of the protagonists in both Nila NorthSun's "Up & Out" and in Nora Naranjo-Morse's "Mud Woman's First Encounter with the World of Money and Business" and the way they navigate in each of the worlds. As depicted in the polished copy of this essay, each character responds to each world in a different way. Mud Woman is left vulnerable to the unfamiliar business world after leaving her treasured reservation life, and NorthSun's speaker nostalgically turns back to the reservation life after trying out the trite city life. In these two works, I can understand the struggle of the individual as each tries to assimilate into a foreign culture. Before taking this class, I had never mulled over the gravity of the struggle that American Indians face today. As they try to hold on to their traditional culture, the city life begins to collide with everything they used to know. They have trouble fully adapting and committing to one world. Other short stories and poems that we read written by many native people caused a shift in my perspective. I was finally getting a personal viewpoint on Native American culture. Slowly, as I began to read works like Sherman Alexie's satirical poem on typical stereotypes of American Indians entitled "How to Write the Great American Indian Novel," my previous misconceptions and images of Native Americans began to crumble—I began to abandon my former image of "Indians" as the collective group I had once learned about in my AP US history class and began to see them as individuals with a story to share. As I explored the in-depth history that belonged to American Indians, I began to feel for the main characters in each of these short stories and poems. This course effectively showed me yet another perspective on modern American Indian life that I had not seen before.

Overall, my portfolio reflects how I changed my entire viewpoint of American Indian culture. This class has broadened my ideas and opinions about this beautiful people. I now know that history from textbooks is more complex than it seems—superficial facts alone cannot describe an entire culture that has many times been left forgotten. I purposefully placed each exhibit in this portfolio so that you can see the progression of ways my perspective has deepened. Through this class I was able to explore a great Nation that I had never really understood.

Victoria Moreira

Professor Weaver

English1102M

22 September 2010

A Struggle between Warring Worlds

There is a point in one's life when an imperative decision needs to be made. There is a time for one to leave his comfortable shelter and venture out into a world of harsh realities. Just as a young adult leaves everything he has ever known for the first time and heads off to college, he approaches a new and unfamiliar world. The familiar world that one leaves behind begins to clash with the new one presented. All of the customs and familiar exchanges between one and his old environment now seem foreign and strangely reminiscent. However, this new culture brings new conflict. To which world does one belong? In Nila NorthSun's "Up & Out" and in Nora Naranjo-Morse's "Mud Woman's First Encounter with the World of Money and Business," two clashing worlds emerge, highlighting the varying approaches that NorthSun's speaker and Naranjo-Morse's Mud Woman take to find which world they belong to.

In "Up & Out" the tension between the two worlds of the now-familiar city life and the reservation life that she is nostalgic for affects the way the speaker navigates through each. This tension is caused by differing values between the two worlds. In the city, the trite society the speaker has succumbed to revolves around money and useless materialism. She explains that although "we made better money . . . it got sucked up by / the city by cable t.v. / by sparklettes water by / lunches in cute places / by drinking in quaint bars / instead of home like we did / on the reservation"

(NorthSun lines 18-25). All of her hard-earned money gets sucked backed into the centrifuge of the city. Living the wasteful high life with "high food high medical /high entertainment" does not help the speaker's original intent of starting a new and better life for herself (lines 16-17). Money is wasted in this vicious cycle in which "[people] made more money than / [they've] ever made before / but felt poorer" (lines 7-9). In the rush of the city-life, the speaker emphasizes the lack of importance in relationships between family and friends because it is intently focused on the material aspect of living. As money drives this society, the simplicity of the reservation life to the speaker becomes more enticing. On the reservation, she concedes that although "we only got one tv channel . . . we visited with relatives more" (lines 30-31). The intimacy between people is long missed. Even though "there was no place to eat on the res / 'cept a pool hall with chips & coke / [and] there was only one movie house in town / & nothing good ever showed," the cost of living was lower and more of one's time was spent with others rather than on working to get a bit of money that ends up being taken away by the city (lines 32-35). Compared to the city life that always seems to revolve around "income tax / hoping to get a little something back" and high spending, NorthSun admits "how I hated living on the reservation/ but now/ it doesn't look so bad" (lines 1-4,45-47). She admits that after a journey of exploring both worlds, she would rather return to the world she has tried to run away from. The simplicity of the reservation calls her back.

In "Mud Woman," the two worlds of the confusing city life and the familiar reservation life collide, leaving Mud Woman vulnerable. Mud Woman, who enters this new buisness-world, is ready to share a part of herself with it, looking to start anew and to start her exploration of the world she belongs to. When she arrives to the gallery to start her journey into the business world, immediately the "center of what [she] knew to be real / was shifting with each moment" (Naranjo-Morse lines 28-29). The two worlds begin to collide. The gallery-owner, whom Mud Woman first meets, represents the materialistic business world that cares only about the superficial and profitable importance of a person when it comes to a business venture. Conversely, Mud Woman, in a genuine way through her mud figurines, represents the unique natural culture and traditions from her reservation life. The business world works in a way that Mud Woman does not understand. In an obtrusive manner, when introducing the rules of society to Mud Woman, the gallery owner arrogantly asks, "First of all dear, do you have a resume? You know, / something written that would identify you to the public" (lines 19-20). As the gallery owner asks Mud Woman about her resume, she plays by the rules of the business world; she only cares about how the public will respond to Mud Woman's artwork. The woman wants "traditional" Indian artwork to sell in her gallery because that is what is profitable—unlike the "strangely different" figurines that Mud Woman makes (line 43). The woman does not believe there is any chance of opportunity for *herself* in Mud Woman's work, yet she buys a few of her pieces because "if for some reason [Mud Woman] make[s] it big, / [she] can be the first to say, 'I discovered you' " (lines 48-49). The gallery owner is purely self-interested and motivated only by profit—ignoring all sense of Mud Woman's feelings. Before she knows it, Mud woman "exchanged her work for the / unexpectedly smaller sum that wholesale prices dictated" (lines 54-55). During the period of this exchange, Mud Woman has no voice—she passively allows the business world to take advantage of her and her artwork. The wholesale prices of the "traditional" Indian artwork in which Mud Woman's work is categorized automatically dictate the value of her work—Mud Woman's unique and careful labor with the way she "concern[ed] herself with the specific curves, bends and / idiosyncrasies, that made each piece her own" is pushed aside for a cheap buy by the business world (lines 4-5). Mud woman, betrayed by this foreign world, realizes that she does not belong to it.

In "Up & Out," the relative distance between the speaker and each world affects the way she responds to the cultures of each. She is familiar with the customs of each world: the way business is conducted and the way the society of city life revolves around the ideas of money and materialism. The way she knowledgeably lists and weighs the negatives of both worlds and reluctantly concedes to rejoining the life of the reservation does not motivate one to feel for her individual circumstance because she is not left vulnerable like Naranjo-Morse's Mud Woman. This stoic distance that is created between the speaker and both of the environments she reflects on collectively holds an emotionally negative connotation. She creates a negative image of both worlds, bluntly listing the reservation's "government commodities [that]. . . tasted like dog food" and the city that "[had] high rent / high food [and] high medical" (lines 36-37, 15-16). Her negative tone creates a cold atmosphere and a detachment in the relationship she has with both environments. Even though there is no emotional connection in the way the speaker ultimately decides that the "reservation doesn't look so bad," the speaker can easily decide which world she wants to belong to because she is informed (lines 45-47). She has experienced both worlds and knows the truths of each.

Conversely in "Mud Woman," the speaker is vulnerable as she experiences and responds to the business world for the first time. She does not know the harsh realities that the business world holds—so different from her familiar customs on the reservation. She has always sold her artwork to those that know her on the reservation, so the customs in that exchange of business are familiar to her. Now, she is lost—prey to a vicious world that thrives on taking advantage of those who are not informed. The reservation life that she is familiar with beckons her home as "she [leaves] the city / and the world of / money and business behind" (Naranjo-Morse lines 71-73). There is an intimate and emotional connection present with Mud Woman as she delves into this unfamiliar world with her heart held humbly open. When the stringent realities of the business world approach, Mud Woman is left defenseless. Now that Mud Woman has experienced both worlds, she returns home to the comfort of what she knows, realizing that the once promising city life is not for her.

Like the speaker in "Up & Out," Mud Woman begins to regret the decision of entering the foreign city life centered around a money-hungry society. Between these clashing worlds, the simplicity of the reservation life prevails. Both MudWoman and NorthSun's speaker realize that the focus of the business world in society is out to get the individual. For Mud Woman, the business world intimately and yet harshly uses her beautiful talent and writes her off with a dollar sign amount that tells her how much she is worth. The clay figurines that are made by the very earth she distinguishes and calls herself by are labeled by a price sticker. After she is cast out of the shop, a part of her is gone—away with her clay figurines. NorthSun's reflections are congruently similar in a more distant manner. She grows tired of the fast and manipulative city life that feeds on the monetary expenditures of unnecessary materialisms. Both regret leaving the peaceful simplicity of the reservation. For both of these women, the reservation will always be a place to call Home.

Works Cited

Naranjo-Morse, Nora. "Mud Woman's First Encounter with the World of Money and Business." *Mud Woman, Poems from the Clay*. Tucson, AZ: University of Arizona Press,1992. 1-3. *Emma.* Web. 21 September 2010.

NorthSun, Nila. "Up & Out." *A Snake in Her Mouth: Poems 1974-96*. Albuquerque, NM: University of New Mexico Press, 1997. 49-50. *Emma.* Web. 21 September 2010.

Background: The time is 1835, and the Cherokee Nation is in crisis. The people are torn on the question of removal. Should the Cherokee people decide to move West now and side with the Ridge faction, or should they fight to stay on their own lands with the Ross faction? In this piece, Elijah Hicks calls the Cherokee people to action. This is his position on removal as seen in an edition of the Cherokee newspaper, The Phoenix.

A LETTER TO THE PEOPLE

by: Elijah Hicks

My friends—brethren in humanity—we stand strong. I beseech you to continue in our fight for justice. Although this tumult continues to burden our hearts, we must labor on until we can keep our lands and see that our future generations flourish on its fruits. However, before us is a great divide among our people. The question of ceding and fleeing from what is rightfully ours remains. Our people, who were once united under one goal, are now fighting against each other like the savages the whites call us. What would our great ancestors, who see our plight, have to say? We cannot win this fight divided. We are as strong as ever before, and we should fight to stay in the lands that are ours.

Our weak brothers, who believe we should flee without a fight, have forgotten who they are. They have forgotten that we were born to live as warriors, not as cowards. The strength that our ancestors have passed on to us is woven into our rooted courage. So, let us remain strong against this unjust removal. We already have become so incredibly united. Courageously, we have turned over the United States Supreme Court and have shown our irrepressible voice as an independent nation. Already our children and people are literate and educated, as we have developed a unified Cherokee writing system and have erected schools for our children to attend. We have cultivated our lands by large-scale farming systems and have become economically successful and independent. We boldly fought the odds and proved every skeptic wrong in their preconceived judgments of our kind. We are innately strong; removal is unnecessary.

The Ridge's, who represent a small minority of the Cherokee, underestimate our strength. They make their point of removal clear, but are we meant to follow in their cowardly footsteps? We are a great nation. We are not a nation of cowards, like this small minority who decide to flee when an obstacle draws near. We are a nation with traditions that move us forward. Are we willing to submit to the whites who have made us their enemies? When will our submission stop? When will their greed cease? We have succumbed to the whites' demands long enough. This unjust submission started long ago with our peaceful ancestors—when "our fathers laid aside their arms and ceded the best portions of their country" even though their act meant nothing.[1] From 1721 until now, more than 120,000 acres of Cherokee land have been ceded, and from more than 22 different treaties our rich soils have been taken from us in attempts to find peace. Our fathers relinquished our rightful lands to avoid aggression. For many years, our people endured manipulation and extortion. When will it end? Georgia has already pushed us beyond its own country's constitutional limits. As witnessed with our fellow Creeks, Georgia has taken its native peoples' rights without their consent. Governor Lumpkin of Georgia so kindly remarks that "the inhumanity of Georgia, so much complained of, is nothing more nor less than the extension of her laws and jurisdiction over this mingled and misguided population who are found within her acknowledged limits."[2] Are our mingled and misguided people wrong not to want to endure the cruelty Georgia has unjustifiably extended over us,

---

1   "Memorial of the Cherokee Nation." *Red Clay, 1835: Cherokee Removal and the Meaning of Sovereignty*. Ed. Jace Weaver and Laura Adams Weaver. 2010. Print. 92.
2   Lumpkin,Wilson. "Speech before Congress." Red Clay, 1835: Cherokee Removal and the Meaning of Sovereignty. Ed. Jace Weaver and Laura Adams Weaver 2010. Print. 84.

after Georgia has flagrantly dehumanized our very identity and has ignored the laws of our Council? Are we too ignorant to know what is best for us? Georgia has already taken away our human liberties. The state claims that it is justified in its actions—even when Georgia made it unlawful "for any person or persons, under colour or pretense of authority from said Cherokee tribe. . . to cause or procure by any means the assembling of any council or other pretended legislative body."[3] If our council is made illegal, how are we to make decisions for the good of our people? Furthermore, Georgia has made it impossible for us to defend ourselves: "no Indian or descendant of any Indian, residing within the Creek or Cherokee Nations of Indians, shall be deemed a competent witness in any court of this State."[4] How are we to defend ourselves in their court system in peaceful and diplomatic ways if they will not allow us?   We cannot endure this injustice any longer. If we passively allow this to continue, our Nation will cease to exist. By fleeing from the problem, we are not ending it. Who is to say that the whites will not further take away our lands after removal? Passivity is no longer an option.

We refuse to go down the dangerous and futile path of removal—not because we are cowards but because it would be suicidal.   As we have witnessed our brothers who have fled earlier, the path was full of disease and death. If we mistakenly listen to those like the Ridge family, we will suffer: even Non-Cherokee people who see these dangerous consequences, like Jeremiah Everts, predict that there will be "much suffering, in the removal of 60.000 souls . . . much exposure, sickness, hunger, [and] nakedness."[5] This is our family. This is our land. This is our life. Let us take care of our people. The demand for removal is unreasonable. We should

3   "Georgia General Assembly." *Red Clay, 1835: Cherokee Removal and the Meaning of Sovereignty*. Ed. Jace Weaver and Laura Adams Weaver. 2010. Print. 61.
4   Ibid. 61
5   Everts, Jeremiah. "'William Penn' Essay." *Red Clay, 1835: Cherokee Removal and the Meaning of Sovereignty*. Ed. Jace Weaver and Laura Adams Weaver. 2010. Print. 55.

not be forced down a path that we do not want to follow. As they push us west of the Mississippi, there is "no guarantee of a new country that could be given to [us]."[6] The land is foreign, and if we are compelled to leave our country, we see nothing but ruin before us, as "the [dark] country west of the Arkansas territory is unknown to us."[7] Most likely, we will hardly get settled in the new location before "[we] will be urged to remove again."[8] How will we survive? When will their greed end? Why must we continue to allow our fate rest in their hands? In a petition sent out by George Lowrey, 13,000 out of 16,000 Cherokee do not want to remove: let us continue to fight for the majority of the Cherokee.

We are strong, and we plan to stay. We will let justice lead us to victory. Our genuine case is simple: "who is the injured, and who is the aggressor? Let conscience answer. . . Do the obligations of justice change with the color of one's skin?"[9] Many of our brothers who have succumbed to the manipulation of justice have lost their way. Our brother Elias Budinot, whose opinion most once trusted when he wrote for *The Phoenix*, once believed in justice. In his own words, he believed that justice would be served—that conscience and truth would be deserved to the Cherokee people. In An Address to the Whites, Budinot simply states in response to the injustice done to us, "Let humanity answer."[10] Can he not remember his original compassion for his people? Have you forgotten yours? We have tried to change ourselves and our traditions for many moons. John

---

6   Ibid. 56

7   "Memorial of the Cherokee Nation." *Red Clay, 1835: Cherokee Removal and the Meaning of Sovereignty*. Ed. Jace Weaver and Laura Adams Weaver. 2010. Print. 94.

8   Everts, Jeremiah. "'William Penn' Essay." *Red Clay, 1835: Cherokee Removal and the Meaning of Sovereignty*. Ed. Jace Weaver and Laura Adams Weaver. 2010. Print. 56.

9   Frelinghuysen, Theodore. "Speech before the Senate." *Red Clay, 1835: Cherokee Removal and the Meaning of Sovereignty*. Ed. Jace Weaver and Laura Adams Weaver. 2010. Print. 72.

10   *Red Clay, 1835: Cherokee Removal and the Meaning of Sovereignty*. Ed. Jace Weaver and Laura Adams Weaver. 2010. Print. 46.

Ross reminds us, in his letter to John C. Calhoun, that "[t]he happiness which [he] once enjoyed, by a quiet & undisturbed ease, in [his] primitive situation before the . . . Civilized Tree . . . [is stained now— planted around] the elysian vallies drenched with blood."[11] Our happiness has ceased. The whites and their policies have changed us. We have tried assimilation. We have allowed them to "civilize" us. We have a proper order of conduct in Council. We are united by blood and are bound by our civilized laws. We have yielded. In our own home, roles are shifting as we assimilate. By changing, we have made excuses for the natural traditions of our culture. In trying to convince the whites of our degree of "civility," those who have abandoned their faith in us, like John Ridge, have begun to degrade us— excusing that "the hardest portion of manual labor is performed by the men, & the women occasionally lend a hand to the field, more by choice and necessity than anything else."[12] Our woman used to work in the fields by choice. But now, under new white societal laws, it is not proper for them to continue in that conduct. Now, we force them to stay in the home and take to a woman's sphere of the white culture. Additionally, a woman's esteem and advice is no longer respected as it once was, as we move from our traditional matriarchy to the white's differing patriarchy. We have become more savage in our ways of assimilation. We have belittled our women and have watched our culture fade. We must reestablish our fate back into our own hands. John Ross adamantly states "all that remains for the Cherokee Nation is to decide for itself whether it will contribute most to [its] own welfare and happiness, for [it] to retain [its] present title to its lands, and remain where [it] is."[13] Let us remain who we are.

---

11   Ross, John. "Letter to John C. Calhoun." *Red Clay, 1835: Cherokee Removal and the Meaning of Sovereignty*. Ed. Jace Weaver and Laura Adams Weaver. 2010. Print. 48.
12   Ridge, John. "'Letter to Albert Gallatin.'"*Red Clay, 1835: Cherokee Removal and the Meaning of Sovereignty*. Ed. Jace Weaver and Laura Adams Weaver. 2010. Print. 32.
13   Ross, John. "Letter to John C. Calhoun." *Red Clay, 1835: Cherokee Removal and the Meaning of Sovereignty*. Ed. Jace Weaver and Laura Adams Weaver. 2010. Print. 48.

We remain strong in numbers. Let our beliefs stand firm. Let our brethren reunite under one kindled flame of unity. We cannot win this battle alone. Without you, our fight is lost, and our life here can be no more. Lost is our history, our ancestors, and our traditions. Is this what you choose?

Elijah Hicks

Humble servant of the people

This is my introductory paragraph of Essay 1 ("A Struggle between Warring Worlds"). This piece best highlights my revision process as it identifies my thoughts and ideas through the pre-write, draft one, draft two and the polished final. Over the course of these revisions, I developed my ideas significantly, reorganized my points in a logical flow, narrowing to my thesis. Developing my thesis is usually the hardest part for me when writing a paper. By creating these drafts, I was able to consolidate the general point of my paper into a solid thesis. As I progressed through my drafts, I developed the direction of my paper more in this first introductory paragraph. By starting my introduction with an out of context example and applying it to the main theme of conflict in that brings together the two works that I am comparing, I show a more clear image of what I mainly want to talk about in my entire paper. Below is my Pre-write, Draft 1, Draft 2, and the Polished Paragraph.

Purple= word choice was changed

Green=elements changed to give a clearer image

Pre-Write

In this stage of my revision, I was just thinking about generating some ideas for my paper in a stream-of-conscious-like manner. This pre-write actually came from a previous journal that talked about my initial reactions to the work itself. Here, I concentrated on Mud Woman's and Naranjo-Morse's perspectives on the two very different worlds they try to belong to. By contrasting these similar themes, I was able to come up with a general guideline for my thesis seen in Draft 1.

"Mud woman's First Encounter with the world of Money and Business" by Nora Naranjo-Morse

She doesn't feel that she belongs in the material city life—Her art is a part of herself and represents who she is. . . sadly, she sells it for a couple of dollars, so someone else can make a profit off of her. She is innocent, naïve, and callow. She is earthly- made from clay like her figurines --her figures are not "traditional" or "Indian-like,", so the shop owner thinks they're useless, but they ARE art and they ARE important because they are unique. She leaves feeling cheated -She has no plans to stay in the city life that betrays/does not accept her the way she is.

- The shop owner represents the material world. She is only concerned with money and a "name."

"Up & Out" by Nila NorthSun

- One makes more money but feels poorer

- One spends more money in the "high life"

- There are no jobs on reservation--- there are less opportunities, so one must go to the city for opportunity.

- Money gets "sucked up by the city"== which is in turn goes to the government (bitter tone against the government).

- In the city people waste money on "cute" but unnecessary things VS. on the reservation government commodities are bad -government doctors are bad but free -even though the reservation is small and doesn't measure up in size/wealth to the city... NorthSun still prefers its simplicity to the city life.

Draft 1 of Paragraph

In this paragraph, I identify my main claim in a general way. I show that in each work the main character is in the process of finding herself in either the Reservation life or the city-life. However, I later realized, after making this draft, that this thesis was not the direction I wanted to pursue. I didn't want to really talk about each woman's struggle of finding her identity as much as finding which world she belongs to. Also, this paragraph is lacking a lot of development. This introductory paragraph is essentially only my thesis statement with no development.

In Nora Naranjo-Morse's poem " Mud Woman's First Encounter with the World of Money and Business" and in Nila NorthSun's "Up & Out," two clashing worlds that emerge through each text highlight the individual's struggle to find her identity in one world or the other.

Draft 2 of Paragraph

In this draft, I better develop my position and introduce elements that I will later expound upon in the rest of my essay. My thesis in this draft is much more focused. My thesis in this draft is highlighted in yellow. *Also in this revision, I began this introductory paragraph (as seen in the green front) with a powerful statement that introduced a general idea about decisions. I then went on to describe an example of the importance of decisions in an individual's life and how they need to be made to solve conflicts. Next, I linked this example to the main characters in both works and their experiences of conflict about the worlds they chose to belong to, analogizing a more accurate image these main characters undergo in each work. I chose to bring these images in from a more general idea to a my specific thesis, progressively narrowing my thesis, and getting the audience to think about the bigger picture.*

There is a point in one's life when an imperative decision needs to be made. There is a time for one to leave his comfortable shelter and venture out into a world of harsh realities. Just as a young adult leaves everything he has ever known for the first time and heads off to college, he approaches a new and unfamiliar world. The familiar world that one leaves behind begins to clash with the new one presented. All of the customs and familiar exchanges between one and his old environment now seem foreign and strangely reminiscent. However, this new culture sweeps in conflict. To which world does one truly belong? In Nila NorthSun's "Up & Out" and in Nora Naranjo-Morse's "Mud Woman's First Encounter with the World of Money and Business," two clashing worlds emerge, highlighting the varying approaches that NorthSun's speaker and Naranjo-Morse's Mud Woman take to find which world they belong to.

Polished Paragraph

Another problem that I always have when revising my drafts is being concise and using correct syntax. In this polished paragraph, I changed a few words (as highlighted in purple) to make my syntax less awkward. Also, for stylistic purposes, I changed the punctuation to better demonstrate that the following clause explains the preceding one.

There is a point in one's life when an imperative decision needs to be made. There is a time for one to leave his comfortable shelter and venture out into a world of harsh realities. Just as a young adult leaves everything he has ever known for the first time and heads off to college, he approaches a new and unfamiliar world. The familiar world that one leaves behind begins to clash with the new one presented. All of the customs and familiar exchanges between one and his old environment now seem foreign and strangely reminiscent. However, this new culture brings new conflict: to which world does one truly belong? In Nila NorthSun's "Up & Out" and in Nora Naranjo-Morse's "Mud Woman's First Encounter with the World of Money and Business," two clashing worlds emerge, highlighting the varying approaches that NorthSun's speaker and Naranjo-Morse's Mud Woman take to find which world they belong to.

I felt that while reviewing this essay I really looked at elements from each individual paragraph and "the bigger picture." My peer had a very unified essay— always coming back to the main idea throughout each of her paragraphs—so I really focused us on helping her add evidence to her commentary and rewording her sentences to make her ideas more concise. This essay demonstrates my best skills as a reviewer because this essay had so much potential. I felt that I did not "edit" this paper but really reviewed it— focusing not on the nit-picky errors, like grammar, but instead on its content and coherence.

Mary Ashford

English 1102M

Professor Laura Weaver

9 November 2010

The Transformation of Female Cherokee Gender Roles

In his *Notes on the State of Virginia,* United States' President Thomas Jefferson states, "' The [Cherokee] women are subjected to unjust drudgery. This I believe is the case with every barbarous people....It is civilization alone which'" corrects this issue (Johnston 39). In other words, President Jefferson believed that the gender roles of Cherokee women were inhumane and must be corrected through civilization programs. Therefore, he enforced these particular programs like his predecessors,

> **Comment:** Maybe start with a topic sentence for the idea of the entire paper... not with evidence (the quote).

> **Comment:** "united states'" is somewhat redundant here... President Thomas Jefferson is sufficient.

which instilled Euro-American values and encouraged Cherokee women to adopt more domestic duties rather than agricultural and political. Because of this, the gender role of Cherokee women slowly began to shift, and their new responsibilities became solidified through the prospects of Cherokee Removal.

> Comment: ?? maybe to make more clear Insert "than those of their once traditional agricultural and political"... Or something like that

> Comment: GOOD INTRO!! clear main idea... maybe you just might want to think about inserting the quote by jefferson later as evidence in a body paragraph and not in the intro of the paper.

Before the influence of the United States, the Cherokee nation was thriving in terms of agricultural growth. This was partly due to the Cherokee's solid establishment of known gender roles. For instance, men consciously knew that their place in the tribe was one of a hunter. They were expected to supply their families with meat to be used in meals and animal skins to be used for clothing. Women, on the other hand, were deemed as farmers. They cultivated the land, planted seeds, and raised the tribe's crops. Ultimately, these given tasks of both Cherokee women and men aided the tribe in terms of consumption and trade, which allowed for the continued growth of the nation.

> Comment: Less passive voice

> Comment: Delete "as"

> Comment: This paragraph needs evidence. it has a lot of commentary...but needs more evidence to support! Add support to this paragraph or merge it with the next one because you're still talking about the same thing. If you merge the two, your next paragraph is full of evidence that supports this previous paragraph--at you can use it to validate the commentary.

Not only did the recognized establishment of Cherokee gender roles add to agricultural growth, but it also contributed to political prowess. Both Cherokee women and men were encouraged to voice their opinion in council meetings. They did this by "speak[ing] one at a time, in a deliberate voice, slowly and calmly." No one interrupted the orators whether they were male or female. Instead, "everyone waited

> Comment: Good support!

politely for the [speaker] to conclude. Then the next [person] would rise and without gestures give his [or her] arguments." Also, women were allowed to decide the fate of captives, participate in treaty negotiations, and sign deeds conveying land titles such as to the Proprietors of Carolina. This inclusion of women in council meetings and other political issues provided the tribe with multiple perspectives, which then allowed the council and native officials to make conscious decisions for the betterment of the Cherokee nation .

However, these particular roles, especially those concerning women, were unacceptable according to the United States. Americans firmly believed that Cherokee women were being treated unfairly. They thought the females were being forced to perform tasks that were not suitable for their gender. For example, women, in compliance to Euro-American values, were not to exhaust their skills in labor outside of the home. This meant that a woman's place was in her household and not in the field. Also, a woman had no business in politics according to this particular Euro-American mindset. A woman's reign only went as far as her home and did not carry on into the decision making process of the nation.

Therefore, the U.S. government and missionaries took it upon themselves to implement what came to be known as Civilization programs.

> **Comment:** Parenthetical needed

> **Comment:** Explain" proprietors of carolina" part... I'm interested... expound!

> **Comment:** Add maybe" according to their own societal rules."

> **Comment:** Merge this paragraph with the next together..... you're talking about the same thing. same problem as before.... this paragraph has no evidence, and you have no topic sentence in the next paragraph.. you start off with evidence. Merge?

These programs instilled Euro-American views of a woman's role in society. More simply, the proponents of "civilization" turned Cherokee "women into housewives" by confining them to the domestic sphere. This was accomplished through the teaching of tribal women on how to upkeep the household, dress appropriately, and act in a lady-like manner. Once instructed, the United States believed that the Cherokee women would become liberated. No longer would they be regarded as slaves in comparison to Cherokee men. Instead, women would be held in higher estimation. In fact, Return J. Meigs, the Cherokee agent in Tennessee at the time, states in his journal that civilization programs allowed Cherokee women to be viewed as delicate creatures in the eyes of man, and "'as esteem and love are concomitant between the sexes, love is becoming a sentimental passion never known in a perfect savage state.'"

Due to these civilization programs implemented by the United States, the gender role of Cherokee women slowly began to change. The majority of women were no longer found working in the fields since now they were not required to farm the land. Also, less women were found present at council meetings since they were no longer expected to voice their opinions over political matters. In fact, these tasks were now taken over by Cherokee males. Thus, women took up housekeeping as their primary concern. While their husband were out farming,

Comment: Parenthetical missing. Check these throughout your paper... I saw that you were missing a few

Comment: Change verbs in quote to flow when integrating

hunting, and attending council meetings, Cherokee women could be found at home, busy taking care of their children and preparing dinner.

> **Comment:** Evidence?? ? merge these paragraphs together And create a new conclusion paragraphs (without quotes). A conclusion should not really be more support of your claim.. it should be more of an overview of your content and your main idea.

This shift in the gender roles of women finally came to a close once Cherokee Removal commenced in the mid 1800's. Due to the passing of the U.S. Cherokee Removal Act, the entirety of the Cherokee nation was forced to move out west for multiple reasons. These reasons included the increasing fear that the Cherokee were becoming too powerful as a nation and the United States' need for more land to satisfy a growing population. Because of this, the Cherokee found these justifications and the situation as a whole quite troubling, so many council meetings were held to discuss the pressing matter of removal. Whereas women beforehand would have taken an active role in this discussion, the majority of them no longer did so, for they believed men to be better suited in solving political issues. Therefore, instead of attending council meetings to talk about the uncertain future of the Cherokee nation, women left those distressing matters up to the men while they were at home taking care of the children and cooking meals. This can be seen in the signing of the Treaty of New Echota in 1835, for only Cherokee men signed this document. This is quite a change in regards to gender roles, for women used to take an interest in important matters that concerned the nation, especially in ones that would relinquish all Cherokee territory in the southeast to the United States government in exchange for land in what would come to be known as Oklahoma. Due to this lack of involvement, the political power of Cherokee women was lost and their new stations in the domestic sphere became a permanent transition.

NEED HELP

---------------> paragraph about why this is all important yes

---------------> conclusion (the above could be your conclusion—ties everything together with no new evidence).

--------------->What format do I use for this paper? Footnotes or Works Cited?

Victoria's revision:
Two strengths:
- Very well unified essay!
- There was an easy flow from ideas—I can easily follow your direction
One thing to work on:
- adding evidence to some paragraphs to show support for the claim of the paragraph. You have a lot of commentary at times... just make sure to add so primary support.

THE PHOENIX

Words from the people

October 1835   Issue No. Seventeen

A Divide Among Our Nation

What is to come at the next council meeting? *Your answers found on page 4 of this issue!*

AN ADDRESS TO STAND UNITED: BY PRINCIPLE CHIEF JOHN ROSS

Brothers:

I make this appeal to my fellow Cherokees in the sake of unity. I know that Chief Ross and the Ridge faction want the same thing: to allow the Cherokee people to live in freedom and happiness away from the greed of the Americans who are taking our land by aggression and force of law. I feel that there is a compromise that would allow us to remain here in our homeland.

Continued on Page 3

AN EDITORIAL ON ELECTIONS: BY ELIAS BUDINOT

We have seen the affects of foreign tyranny and have faced its frustrations on a daily basis. It is enough for our nation to deal with, without the added effects of a tyrant in our midst.

Continued on Page 2

A Letter from the Editor:

Brothers, our fight stands strong. I beseech you to continue in our fight for justice. Although this tumult continues to burden our hearts, we must labor on until we can keep our lands and see that our future generations flourish on its fruits. However, before us is a great divide among our people. The question of ceding and fleeing from what is rightfully ours remains. Our people, who were once united under one goal, are now fighting against each other like the savages the whites call us. What would our great ancestors, who see our plight, have to say? We cannot win this fight divided. The Ridges make their point loud and clear—but are we *meant* to follow in their cowardly footsteps?

Continued on Page 4

THE PHOENIX   PAGE **2**

Viewpoints from the People

REPRESENTATIONS FROM THE ROSS AND RIDGE FACTIONS

The compromise is simple: we should divide our Cherokee lands amongst ourselves and give the remainder to the whites.

The Cherokee lands we currently occupy contain roughly 30,000 square miles. Accordingly, if each man, woman and child of the Cherokee nation – 16,500 strong – were given one square mile each, the whites could take the remaining 13,500 square miles and do with it as they wish. What can we do with those 640 acres? We can farm, raise livestock and earn a living for ourselves, our wives and children.

Some of our Cherokee brothers left many years ago for lands in Arkansas. The lands are barren, without water and without rich soil on which to grow the food that makes us strong. How can one live without food or water? Or how can one protect himself against combatting and foreign tribes? The whites said they would protect those Cherokees and honor their claims to those lands, but instead they were betrayed. I have heard that land is growing increasingly cramped as others of our red brothers are torn from their lands and forced to live there. The whites say they it will take them forty generations to reach the western

ocean. But they have already made it to Arkansas, half way across this great land, in three! In forty years the whites will either have us completely surrounded, or will continue to remove us. If we capitulate now they will realize that the Cherokee people can be bought for a price and moved at their behest. They do not care; they will be happy to push us so far that we will be forced to live in that western ocean and drown. Removal will assure our people the watery grave of which I speak.

I appeal to you, my Cherokee brothers to unify together and resist removal. Chief Ross and the Ridges must listen to the voice of the people.

Signed,
Robert Adair - Member, Cherokee National Council

An Editorial on Elections
by Elias Budinot continued...

We have seen the affects of foreign tyranny and have faced its frustrations on a daily basis. It is enough for our nation to deal with, without the added effects of a tyrant in our midst. John Ross has been a strong and noble leader for these past seven years, avidly fighting for his nation. He, however, has made

the decision to stifle the voice of the people he has promised to hear. This despotic behavior is not helping our struggling nation. Ross accuses John Ridge and his followers of dividing the nation, but for centuries, our culture has been based around discussion and equal voice. This blatant disregard of our laws will ultimately be more divisive than adhering to tradition and allowing our voices to be heard. It should be up for the people to decide who is most apt to lead them into the next phase of progress.

John Ross does not represent the only opinion of our people. There is another position that has been gradually growing might as people come to realize what we are really facing. John Ridge has been a compassionate leader amongst our people. I support him as my brother and leader, for he has only the best interests of our great nation at heart. The only way to guarantee that the people are being best represented is to reinstate election. Fairness and reason must stand. Ross's actions have been neither fair nor reasonable. Their leader cannot silence the Cherokee Nation.

Pro-Removal
by John Ridge

We are surrounded by people that want to do us harm and break our nation apart. But we have been given a way out, a way to keep our nation and our people intact: the proposal for removal offered by the United States. While this may seem to be counterintuitive, it is the only logical position. The man who holds U.S. power in his hands is President Andrew Jackson. He in no way wishes to allow us to stay on our lands and will not stand in the way of anything that threatens us. Some suggest that we simply wait until a new President comes into office to replace Jackson. This seems to me a false attempt to throw the problem into the future; we have no guarantee of positive improvement in the temperament of the president. In any case, our nation and our people cannot wait that long.

We have seen over and over what has happened to people in our position. While some may argue that others have made their stand, there is not a single case of success in the situation we find ourselves of any armed resistance. We find ourselves surrounded and outnumbered, with little ability to fight a war in the shadows as the Seminole have done, not sharing their way of life or resources. This option ends only in destruction. We are at an unprecedented point, where someone that could take everything from us has offered a price for what they would take by force if refused. We can move now to somewhere outside of white control and make our nation stronger and better.

Concerns from George Lowrey
Another topic of discussion that aids in the support of Indian non-removal goes back to the well-known case of *Worcester v. Georgia*. In 1832, this case gave us Cherokee entitlement to federal protection, and the U.S. Government now controls us Indians. Therefore, how can Georgia try to tell us Cherokee that we must leave? They possess no right to do this. Although Jackson claims, "It puts an end to all possible danger of collision between the general and state governments on account of the Indians," it is made very clear in *Worcester* that the state government does not have control over the Cherokee nation. Forcefully pushing us out will do nothing but cause ruckus and chaos in which the state and country do not need. Just as Principal Chief Ross says, it is undoubtedly desirable for everyone that the Government "...should adopt some other means to satisfy Georgia."2 Why must Georgia force us Indians out if we were here first? Or better yet, if the land out West is so promising, why can't the Georgians migrate there themselves? Why must violence be created for no reason?

Promising words
by Principle Chief John Ross
continued. . .

How is it that in the land of our ancestors, we are being oppressed and denied our rights to sovereignty? We are not the savages that the United States thinks we are. The Cherokee Nation has our own written language which is featured in our own newspaper, The Cherokee Phoenix, which also prints in English as well. Our government has become more democratic and model after that of the United States. By Western standards, we have advanced quite a bit from our "uncivilized ways" or so it should be. No matter how

THE PHOENIX

seems that we have not come far enough. We probably will never be as civilized as they want us to be; civilized in that it is a subjective label placed on people by others. Let us keep in mind who we are and what we have come from. We are the Cherokee.

When our ancestors came to this land, they planned that their children would live together just as they did. We would have everything we would need, and we would all work as one for the better of the Cherokee Nation. However, external forces like Georgia and President Jackson are working against us.

Simply put, they want us all out. Although some of us may be very skeptical of our ability to accomplish staying in our land, by working together and using practical means we will be able to keep what is ours. We have the right to stay, to govern ourselves under the unity of our nation, and to have peaceful relations with the U.S. and Georgia.

There have been various offers made to our nation regarding removal. It has been attempted to buy our land out for amounts of money that are unsuitable to support the nation. There is more gold in our land than what they offered us in money. The main aspect of this removal is emigration from Georgia and relocation into the strange lands of the West. In letters from our brothers and sisters there, the land is nothing like ours. It lacks trees and water, for which we are very dependent. How could we ever trade our fertile lands for a lot of sand that is too far away from that which our ancestors passed on to us?

Let us remember the interest of our entire nation, not of radical minorities. This is our home. Let us unite to keep it that way.

Continued Letter from the Editor...

We are not a nation of cowardice. We are a nation with traditions that move us forward. Are we willing to submit to the whites who have made us their enemies? When will our submission stop? When will *their* greed cease? We have succumbed to the white's demands long enough. This unjust submission started long ago with our peaceful ancestors —when our fathers laid aside their arms and ceded the best portions of their country even though it meant nothing. For many years, our people endured manipulation and extortion. When will it end? Georgia has already pushed us beyond its own country's constitutional limits. As witnessed with our fellow Creeks, Georgia has taken its native peoples' rights without their consent. Governor Lumpkin of Georgia so kindly illustrates that the inhumanity of Georgia, so much complained of, is nothing more nor less than the extension of her laws and jurisdiction over this mingled and misguided population who are found within her acknowledged limits. Are our *mingled* and *misguided* people wrong to not want to endure the cruelty Georgia has unjustifiably extended over us? Are we too ignorant to know what is best for us? If we passively allow this to continue, our Nation will cease to exist. Passiveness is no longer an option.

So which path do we take? The one of courage or fear? Our weak brothers who believe we should flee without a fight *have forgotten who they are*. The strength that our ancestors have passed onto us is innately woven into our rooted courage. We were born to live as warriors not to die as cowards.

Elijah Hicks
Humble servant of the people

At the next Council Meeting...
President Jackson has further refused us of our rightful annuity payments because the proposal for elections did not pass. His continuous bribes continue to manipulate every order of rightful Cherokee business.

Appendix

LEARNING (YOUR FIRST JOB)

by Robert Leamnson, PhD

Introduction (Don't skip this part)

These pages contain some fairly blunt suggestions about what to do in college. Some of them may seem strange to you, some might seem old fashioned, and most will come across as labor intensive. But they have worked very well for many students over the past 20 years, since the first edition came out. This edition is more up to date, but the basic message has not changed much.

A fundamental idea that you will encounter over and again, is that learning is not something that just happens to you, it is something that *you do to yourself*. You cannot be "given" learning, nor can you be forced to do it. The most brilliant and inspired teacher cannot "cause" you to learn. Only you can do that. What follows are some fairly explicit "learning activities" or behaviors, but they are all *your* activities, and now and then those of your fellow students. But there is also a basic assumption underlying these ideas, and that's that you do want to learn something while getting a diploma. Without that desire, nothing will work.

Some words we need to understand

It happens, too often, that someone reads a passage or paragraph, as you are, and gets an idea very different from what the writer intended. This is almost always because the reader has somewhat different meanings for the words than did the writer. So that we don't have that problem here I'll make clear the meanings I intend by the words I use. We'll start with:

Learning

While few people think of it this way, learning is a biological process. It is indeed biological because thinking occurs when certain webs (networks) of neurons (cells) in your brain begin sending signals to other webs of neurons. You, of course, are not conscious of this process, but only of the thought that results. But there is no doubt that thinking is the result of webs of cells in your brain sending signals to other webs.

How can knowing what causes thought help in the learning process? Start by considering that human learning has two components:

1) Understanding

2) Remembering

Either of these by itself is not sufficient. Knowing a bit about how the brain works when you're thinking will help you to see why *both* understanding and remembering are necessary for learning.

Anytime you encounter a new idea (and that, after all, is why you are in college) you need to "make sense" of it, or, to understand it. And if you are actually *trying* to make sense of it, your brain is firing a lot of webs of neurons until one or more of them "sees" the logic or causality in a situation. Understanding sometimes comes in a flash and we feel, "Oh, I get it!" Other times it takes repeated exposure or the use of analogies until we finally "get it." But if we *never* get it, then we still don't understand—we haven't tried enough circuits in the brain.

So, right from the beginning, making sense of what you read or hear involves focused attention and concentration, in other words, "brain work." I'm confident that almost all college students "could" understand what is required of them by focusing attention on what is being read or heard, and stick with it until the thoughts in their heads pretty much matched those of the speaker or writer.

Unhappily, this is not the way all students in college behave. The most frequent complaint I hear from college instructors is that too many of their students are simply "passive observers."

So the big rule about understanding is that it *cannot* be achieved passively. It demands an active and focused mind.

Some very bright students find little difficulty in understanding what they hear or read. But some of these smart people get very poor grades and sometimes drop out. The reason is, they neglect the second part of learning, which is *remembering*.

For most people, I suspect, remembering is more difficult than understanding. I would suggest that this is because few people know much about memory, or that it is likewise a biological process involving the firing of webs of neurons in the brain. Most people think of memories as ideas, pictures, or events that are lodged somewhere in their heads, and these places simply need to be "found." The fact, however, is that memories are not things always present somewhere in our heads. Memories must be *reconstructed* each time they are remembered. This reconstruction, in biological terms, means firing up almost the same webs of neurons that were used to perceive the original event. This would seem to be easy, but it is not in most cases. Here's the reason.

Use it or lose it

These webs I've been speaking of are networks of connected neurons. The details do not need to be understood, but the fact is, the *connections* between brain cells are not necessarily permanent. *Much of our brain is not hard wired.* One can think of neurons as having a big, important rule, "if the connection I made gets used a lot, it must be doing something important or useful, so I will strengthen the connection so it doesn't fall apart." And that's exactly what it does (even though, in fact, it itself doesn't *know* what it's doing.) Now the bad news. If a neuron makes a connection that does not get used (no matter how useful it *might have been*) it breaks the connection and it's probably gone forever. In short, neural circuits that get used become stable, those that do not get used fall apart.

So it is that we can understand something quite clearly, and some time later not be able to remember what it was we understood. The biological explanation is that the "web of understanding" was not used enough to become stable, so it fell apart.

If you've followed all of this you probably see the bad news coming. If learning means *both* understanding and remembering, we have to *practice* what we understand. Without rehearsal, that fantastic circuitry that enabled our understanding will gradually disintegrate and we can no longer reconstruct what we once understood.

> If learning means both understanding and remembering, we have to practice what we understand.

Some readers are no doubt wanting to get on to the "tricks" for getting high grades. But for a lot of college courses, getting a high grade involves *only* one trick—learn the material. Learning, as described here, is the trick that always works.

Learning is the goal—keep that always in mind through the rest of these pages. Grades will take care of themselves.

The Classroom

The classroom might be very traditional—a collection of students in chairs and an instructor at the front—or people seated at computer terminals, or alone at home with the computer. So long as these are in some way "interactive" with an instructor, the following suggestions will be valid and useful.

The reason something must be said about so commonplace a thing as the classroom is that too many students see it incorrectly and so they waste a highly valuable occasion for learning. The most common misconception is that the class period is that occasion when the instructor tells you what you need to know to pass the tests. Seen this way, it can only be a dreary thing, and from this perception flow a number of bad habits and behaviors that make learning more laborious and less interesting that it can be and should be.

"Taking" notes

I would like to see the expression "taking notes" removed from the vocabulary and replaced with one often used in Great Britain, that is "making notes." "Taking" implies a passive reception of something someone else has made. It too often consists of copying what's on a chalkboard or being projected on a screen.

Copying from a projected image is usually quite difficult and trying to copy what someone is saying is nearly impossible. Attempts to take notes in this way produces something that is usually quite incomplete, often garbled and has the awful effect of turning off the *listening* part of the brain. We are not capable of focusing attention on two different activities at the same time. So we miss what an instructor is saying while we concentrate on writing what he has already said, or copying from the board or screen. Some instructors compensate by making notes *for* the students and passing them out. This practice can help the better students—those who already know how to learn—but for many others it only makes matters worse. For a passive person, having a set of teacher-prepared notes means that they now have *nothing* to do during the class period. So they just sit, or daydream, or doze off, and often quit coming to class altogether. Why not, if it's all in the notes? Two more definitions will help to see that this is a recipe for failure.

Information and Knowledge

Even college professors and authors of books often confuse these words or use them interchangeably. In fact they mean very different things. Let's start with information. The world is awash in information. All the books in the library have information, as do journals, magazines, and the uncountable number of websites and postings on the internet. All of this information is transferable from one medium to another, sometimes with lightening speed. *None of it, however, is knowledge!* The reason being that knowledge can only exist in someone's head. Furthermore, the expression "transfer of knowledge" is ridiculous because it describes the impossible.

This might be a novel or surprising idea so let's examine it further. Suppose your chemistry teacher has a correct and fairly thorough knowledge of oxidation/reduction reactions. Can this knowledge be transferred to you? How wonderful if it could be. Something like a "transfusion" or "mind meld" and you know instantly what he/she knows! None of that is possible. All your teacher can give you is *information*, and perhaps the inspiration for you to do your part. This information is always in the form of symbols. These symbols might be words,—spoken or written—numbers, signs, diagrams, pictures, and so on. You cannot learn anything unless you have previous knowledge of the meaning of the symbols. As a clear example, you cannot learn from someone speaking Farsi if you know only English, no matter how accurate and useful the information embedded in that language. This idea—new knowledge depends greatly on prior knowledge—will come up again later.

But if, happily, you can indeed "make sense" of new information on chemical reactions (or anything else) you can then construct your own knowledge by using the new information and incorporating it into your prior knowledge base. But, as noted above, this will involve using some not-used-before neural connections, so if you want to *remember* what you now *understand*, you must practice, that is review a number of times, or use the new knowledge repeatedly to solve problems or answer questions. Remember the rule about new knowledge—use it or lose it.

> **Remember the new rule about knowledge - use it or lose it.**

So, what do I have to do?

All of this talk about brains, information, and knowledge is not just abstract theory. It *is* the way we learn. The way to learn, then, is to align your own activities with those behaviors we already know will work.

Time

Time is nothing at all like the way we talk about it. How often do you hear someone say that they "didn't have time?" It's a perfectly meaningless expression. When you wake up on a Sunday morning, you have exactly 168 hours of time until the following

Sunday morning. And everybody on the planet gets 168 hours. *No one ever has any more or any less time than anyone else!* Time cannot be "found," nor "stretched," nor "compressed," nor "lost." It cannot be "saved" or "bought," or in any other way "managed" for any realistic meaning of the word "manage." So why do we use all these meaningless expressions? It's because they let us avoid the embarrassing process of examining our priorities, a ranked list of those things we hold to be important. Sleeping is a high priority for everyone—it's a biological necessity, like food—so we all spend a fair amount of our allotted time blissfully unconscious. Now, what about the rest of our 168 hours? For someone who has to work part time to meet expenses, work is a high priority activity and they show up on schedule and on time because losing the job would mean losing the income and the consequences would be serious. So, after sleeping, eating, working, and, one hopes, going to classes, the rest of our 168 hours are spent doing whatever we find personally important. For some, doing assignments, reading books, writing reports and the like are important, so they always get done. For some others, TV, "hanging out," the internet, and partying are of primary importance, and sometimes they fill up so many of the 168 hours available that there is nothing left at the end of the

week. Remember, no one gets more than 168 hours, so anyone who thinks they can "do it all" is *always* going to "run out of time."

It's your priorities and not the clock that will determine the outcome of your college experience. If it's really important, it will always get done, and always at the expense of the less important.

Studying

You and your teachers will use the word "study" frequently, and always assuming that it means the same thing to everyone. But it doesn't. For way too many college students, particularly in the first year, study never happens until just before a test. Teachers are amazed at the idea, but many students simply see no reason to study if there is no test on the horizon. So here in a nutshell is a most serious misunderstanding between college teachers and beginning students. For teachers, the purpose of study is to understand and remember the course content; for students the purpose of study is to pass the tests.

Now in an ideal world these would amount to the same thing. But in the real world, unfortunately, you can pass some tests without learning much at all. This is not the place for me to beat up on my colleagues, but some do produce truly simple-minded exams that do not require much by way of preparation. So here's an absolutely *heroic* idea if you find yourself bored with a class; try learning more than the teacher demands. Wake up your childhood curiosity and ask why other people find this discipline so interesting that they spend their lives at it. I can about guarantee that there are bright, articulate, and interesting writers in every college discipline. Find a good book and read. That way you'll learn something even if the teacher doesn't demand it.

But such "gut" courses might be rare in your college. The ones that cause trouble and hurt the grade point average are those where the teacher expects serious learning, but leaves most of it up to you. How do you cope with that?

Tough Courses

What makes a course tough? Well, sometimes it only means large amounts of material, many pages to read, lots of writing assignments, and the like. But the really tough course is one where the subject itself is complex, or presents difficult problems for

the learner to deal with, and often goes faster than students would find comfortable. Suppose we add to that a super-smart teacher, but one who simply assumes you know how to learn, and sprays information like a fire hose. For a typical first year student this is the famous "worst case scenario." The whole purpose of my writing is to help you cope with worst case scenarios.

> If you find yourself bored with a class, try learning more than the teacher demands.

During the Lecture

In these tough courses the first idea you must abandon is that you can sit, "take" notes, and worry about it later. Here's another key idea to bring with you to every lecture period. *Worry about it **now***.

You can look upon your teacher as an adversary, something that stands between you and a diploma, but that's a defeatist and erroneous idea. It's better to think of the instructor as your private tutor. Most teachers welcome a considered question on the content. They nearly all resent questions like, "is this going to be on the test?" You don't do yourself any favors by giving your teachers the impression that you're a lazy goof off trying to slide by with minimal effort. Teachers can often pack a wealth of important information in what just sounds like an interesting story. They do not seem to be "giving notes." It's a serious mistake to get comfortable and daydream. When notes are not "given," then you have to make them, and that's anything but relaxing. It takes careful listening, concentration, and a focused mind to pick out the important nuggets from what appears to be a non-stop verbal ramble. A casual remark like, "there are several reasons we believe these things happen," is a clear clue that something worth knowing is coming. As noted, some teachers may pass out notes that they have made, and these might contain an outline of what's important. A fair number of college faculty have learned that this only encourages passivity and cutting classes. (It's quite easy to get the notes from someone else, and if it's only the notes that are important, why spend time sitting in a classroom?) Some teachers have discovered that students can only be prodded to serious mental activity if they *don't* provide prepared notes. This might seem mean spirited to you, but they're just trying to activate your brain.

> Here's another strange but important truth; all of your interests had to be learned.

Under conditions described above, you, to make notes from which you can learn, have to be attuned to what's being said. Not every sentence that drops from an instructor's mouth is going to contain some pearl of wisdom. Much of it is "filler"—rephrasing, giving examples, preparatory remarks for the next point and so on. You have to learn quickly where the gems are. Sentences you hear stay in the short term, immediate recall part of your brain for only a couple seconds. During that brief time you have to make the decision as to whether you've heard something important or just filler. If it was important you have to get the gist into your notes, even if that means not being quite so attentive so far as listening goes. Once it's down, refocus and wait for the next useful idea.

In short, teachers who do not "make it easy" by doing all the work, are, in fact, doing you a favor. What is often called "deep learning," the kind that demands both understanding and remembering of relationships, causes, effects and implications for new or different situations simply *cannot be made easy*. Such learning depends on students actually *restructuring* their brains and that demands effort.

Such learning can, however, be most satisfying and enjoyable, even as it demands effort. I always think of serious learning of any academic subject as being something like practice for a sport or with a musical instrument. No one is born with a genetic endowment for playing either the trombone or ice hockey. These are both *developed* skills and both take long periods of concentration and effort. Both are simply difficult, but how satisfying they are as small elements are learned and burned into our brain circuits! How enjoyable to become proficient! It's exactly the same with academic matters. Give it a try.

About Interests

An obvious response to the thoughts just expressed might be, "but I like hockey, I have no interest in history," or chemistry—whatever. That may well be true, but what is *not true* is the assumption that these interests are natural—something you came into the world with. Here's another strange but important truth; *all of your interests had to be learned!* This is a small example of a paradox. You need to *know something* about a musical instrument, or a sport, or indeed, an academic subject, before you can judge whether or not it's interesting. But if you hold the belief that you cannot learn anything *until* or *unless* it's interesting, then you can never get started on anything new.

I was always impressed with my senior biology majors who came to my office and got around to talking about their courses in psychology, or philosophy, or art history. These students gave every discipline a chance to prove itself. Instead of depending on a teacher to "make it interesting," they studied it on their own to discover why other folk found it interesting enough to write books about it, and teach it in college. You would do yourself a great favor by developing this "curiosity habit" as early on as you can.

Between Classes

When a teacher happens not to assign some specific work to be done for the next period, a disturbing number of beginning students simply assume that means that nothing at all needs to be done. And it so happens that a lot of college instructors *do not assign* each time some reading, or writing, or problem solving to be done. And if you had an orientation session, someone probably told you that "they" expected you to spend three hours on each of your subjects, *for each hour in class!* That usually comes to an amazing 45 hours a week. Most students find that unreasonable and unnecessary, and I tend to agree. But the proper response to an excessive demand is not to do *nothing*. A huge number of new college students, when told to *study* but given nothing specific to do, simply do nothing. So here are some realistic suggestions for study outside class time.

Fill in the Notes

As noted above, it's essential during a lecture to produce some record, no matter how sketchy, of what was presented during that period. A most useful and highly recommended way so spend half an hour or so of study time is to make sense of these notes, and most importantly, turn lists and key words into real sentences that rephrase what went on. When memory fails, that's the time to use resources. Sometimes your best resource is the textbook. Even if no pages were assigned directly, there is a very high probability that the text contains, somewhere, a good, or better, description of what the teacher had presented. You may have to search for it, but tables of contents, chapter headings and the index will lead you to what you need.

Now, read with the intent of re-discovering what was presented in class. Read with understanding as the goal (this will *feel* different than reading because it was assigned.) People who know the education process thoroughly say that *most* learning in

college goes on outside the classroom. So it is that you will know *more* about the day's material after this "filling in" process than when you first heard it.

But there is a further critical element here. You must *write* in your notes, in real sentences, what you have learned by the reading. Writing has an enormous power to *fix* things in the mind. *Always* write what you have learned. (Once in a while a short paragraph that summarizes or paraphrases an important aspect becomes exactly what you need on an exam. You will almost certainly remember it because you've already written it before.) There are two other good resources for filling in the notes should the textbook be insufficient. These are your classmates and the teacher (or tutor if one is available.)

Huge studies have been done to find out just what "works" for college students. What, in other words, did the truly successful students actually *do* that the unsuccessful ones did not? The first of the two most outstanding findings was that successful students had gotten "connected" to those of their teachers who were open to talking with students (and there are a lot of these.) The intent was not merely social. The point was to become more familiar with course content by simply discussing it with an expert.

Remember, the successful students said that this was the *most important* thing they did to be successful. So you don't have to wonder about it; the experiment's already been done.

The second most important activity for success was to form small study groups, or pairs, with the express purpose of talking about the course content, their notes, and assigned work. Working together on assignments and problems is not cheating. Copying without learning is cheating. Discussing the details of an assignment or problem is just cooperative learning—one of the most useful habits you can develop in college. (I'm perfectly aware, by the way, that getting some guys together to discuss psychology sounds like a pretty "nerdy" thing to do. Well, so what? Really smart college students have no problem stealing a page from the "Nerd's Handbook" if it means learning more and doing better.)

Assignments

Here again, attitude will influence how you react to assigned work. To view it as paying dues, or taxes, or as mere busywork that teachers insist on out of habit, is to squander an excellent learning opportunity. Inexperienced students see assignments as something to be *done*; experienced students see them as something to be *used*. Look on every assignment as a clue from the teacher—what he or she considers important enough to spend time learning. Assignments, in most cases, are solid, meaty chunks of what's important. Don't just *do* assignments with minimal effort and thought, *use* them to learn something new.

Always write what you have learned.

Thoughts on verbalization

Here's another experiment that's already been done and you won't have to repeat. Things do not go into memory as a result of thinking about them vaguely—in the abstract. It has been well documented that *thought*, to be useful, must be *verbal*. Now all that means is that, to be remembered, and so useful, your thought on a topic needs to be either spoken, aloud, to another person, or written on paper. (Recall the earlier idea that information can only *move* by means of symbols, words spoken, signed, or written.) In either case, good English sentences are needed—not just word clusters. You need *verbs*. Who did what to whom? How does this thing cause that thing to happen? These facts support the suggested need to talk to teachers and classmates and use writing assignments to say what's true or useful. And here's a bonus! If you have filled in your notes and discussed a topic with a classmate, even if it only took 30 minutes, you will be *prepared* for the next class. That means you will have something to say should there be a "pop quiz," or if the teacher starts asking questions. Or, just as well, you can start the class by asking a well-prepared question on the last period's material. Trust me—the teacher will notice, and remember, favorably.

> Learn as you go means you're always prepared.

Access and high technology

There have been some noisy claims that today's students will turn out to be the best educated so far, *because* they have access (by way of the internet) to unimaginably more information than any previous generation. I have reservations about this claim for several reasons. For one thing, the internet has been with us for quite some time, and those of us who teach college are still looking for the promised improvement. Results should have showed up by now.

The principal reason, however, goes back to the fundamental difference between *information* and *knowledge*. Knowledge is what has the potential for improving the individual and society. But websites are completely devoid of knowledge; all they have is information (and not all of that is reliable!) No matter how many websites you have access to, none of them can do anything for you unless you can make sense of (and evaluate) what you find there.

And here is another little paradox I discovered by observing the differences between accomplished college seniors and most first year students. Instead of getting knowledge from the internet, *you need to have a lot of knowledge beforehand* to make sense of the ocean of information you find there.

It's tempting to believe that access to more information is going to make college easy. But it's just a temptation. You fall for it at your peril. The internet is a tool, and a very useful one, but as with all tools, you have to be knowledgeable to use it profitably.

Exams

I have intentionally put last what most new college students consider to be the single most important aspect of college—tests and exams. My reason for this approach is simple. If you attend class regularly, listen with attention, make the best notes you can, fill them in later (preferably with a study partner or two), verbalize your thoughts, and use assignments as learning tools, then you would be ready for a test at any time. Learn as you go means you're always prepared.

That is, of course, a bit overstated. In the real world, a "big test" in the offing makes even the best student nervous, and everyone bears down to some degree to get prepared. For someone who has done it all wrong, whose notes are just words copied without context or explanation, who does nothing between classes, and who never discusses coursework with anyone, and who does assignments thoughtlessly— just to have something to pass in—an upcoming exam is justifiably terrifying. It's these students who do everything wrong who ask embarrassing questions like, "What's this test going to cover?" or, "What chapters should we study?" They're clueless and they know it.

But let's assume you've done all the right things. You still want to do the best you can, and that means review, because stuff tends to slip out of memory, particularly when you have three or four other classes to attend to. But I mean "review" literally. It means learn again, not learn for the first time. No one can "learn" the content of 15 or 20 lectures in two days. Unless it's all completely trivial, that just can't be done. Learning a second time (real review), on the other hand, is a snap compared to learning from scratch. So, review for an exam *should not be stressful*. If you're in a state of panic because of an exam it's because you've been doing the wrong things all along.

But you're smart. You've done the right things. How do you do the review?

Don't go it alone

If you've done the right things you already have a study partner or two. Schedule firm times and places to spend an hour or so reviewing. Estimate how many days it will take to review all the material and get an early start. Don't worry about reviewing too far in advance of the exam! If you talk about the content and *write* summary paragraphs or descriptions, make labeled diagrams, or solve problems on paper, you won't forget— it's guaranteed. Remember, stealing a "nerd trick" will make you a better student.

Get Satan behind thee

The absolute worst thing you can do is to fall for the crazy notion that the way to prepare for an exam is to compress it all in the last 12 to 18 hours before the test, and keep it up right to the very last minute. I could always predict with great accuracy who was going to do poorly on an exam. They were red-eyed, gulping coffee to stay awake, and frantically flipping pages even as the test papers were being distributed. They had done it all wrong.

"Pulling an all-nighter," as the cute expression has it, is based on the completely erroneous belief that the only thing that college work requires is short term memory. Were that true, "last minute" study would make at least some sense. But the truth is, most college work demands thinking about, and using, a storehouse of information firmly lodged in long term memory. "All-nighter" students can usually recall a lot of terms and certain "facts," but can't do anything with them.

Remember, your thinking and remembering are functions of your brain, and that's a biological organ, and significantly, it's one with limited endurance. In short, it becomes less efficient the longer you put demands on it without rest. Trying to study 12

> Trying to study 12 hours without sleep has the same effect on your brain as trying to play basketball for 12 straight hours would have on the rest of your body.

hours without sleep has the same effect on your brain as trying to play basketball for 12 straight hours would have on the rest of your body.

So, a final rule: "Always get a night of restful sleep the night before an exam." Some students are afraid of this rule. They are afraid that sleep will somehow wipe out all they've been studying. But it doesn't! It's another of those things that have been researched and the results are consistent. There is, in fact, a small but significant increase in the ability to recall or reconstruct when learning is followed by sleep. So if you want your brain in tip-top condition for an exam (and who wouldn't?) do your reviewing in one or two hour periods spread out over several days, and get a real night's sleep before the exam.

During the exam

I've heard students, going into an exam, say, "I've done my part; it's out of my hands now." That idea betrays the erroneous notion that all the hard work is done in advance, and during the exam you just pour out what you've learned. Well, sometimes. But exams in the tough courses often shock beginning students because they can't find much that looks familiar. There's a reason, and a solution.

Demanding teachers prepare exams that require performance, where performance is much more than recall. A lot of college instructors produce what might be called "application questions" for their exams. All that means is that you can't just write what you know, you have to use what you know to answer a question or solve a problem that you haven't seen before. Only a malicious teacher would question students on material that had never been discussed, assigned, or included in required reading. It seldom happens. So when seeing something that looks unfamiliar, convince yourself that it's only a question that is asking you to apply something you already know. So it is that concentration and focused thinking are often just as necessary during an exam as before it. If you have learned well, and reviewed properly, you can be confident that you have the necessary knowledge. It just takes some hard thinking to see how it applies to a particular question.

A Summary

No one learns unless they want to. I have assumed here that you do. But learning is a biological process that relies on the brain, a physiological organ that demands the same maintenance the rest of you does. Don't abuse it. The best ways to learn have already been discovered, there's no need for you to rediscover them by making a lot of old mistakes all over again. So it is that what you read here might be disappointing. Instead of new tricks or clever ways to beat the system, it says learning is the only way, and that learning is difficult and requires effort. But we do know how to do it, and when it's done right, it is marvelously satisfying.

I wish all readers of these pages the best of luck in their college days. But as I do so, I'm reminded of the words of the biologist Pasteur who said, "Chance favors the prepared mind."

Robert Leamnson
Dartmouth MA Dec. 2002

HOW IS COLLEGE DIFFERENT FROM HIGH SCHOOL?

FOLLOWING THE RULES IN HIGH SCHOOL	CHOOSING RESPONSIBLY IN COLLEGE
High school is mandatory and usually free.	College is voluntary and expensive.
Your time is structured by others.	You manage your own time.
You need permission to participate in extracurricular activities.	You must decide whether to participate in co-curricular activities.
You can count on parents and teachers to remind you of your responsibilities and guide you in setting priorities.	You must balance your responsibilities and set priorities. You will face moral and ethical decisions you have never faced before.
Each day you proceed from one class directly to another, spending 6 hours each day--30 hours a week--in class.	You often have hours between classes; class times vary throughout the day and evening and you spend only 12 to 16 hours each week in class.
Most of your classes are arranged for you.	You arrange your own schedule in consultation with your adviser. Schedules tend to look lighter than they really are.
You are not responsible for knowing what it takes to graduate.	Graduation requirements are complex, and differ from year to year. You are expected to know those that apply to you.
Guiding principle: You will usually be told what to do and corrected if your behavior is out of line.	**Guiding principle:** You are expected to take responsibility for what you do and don't do, as well as for the consequences of your decisions.

How is College Different from High School?

GOING TO HIGH SCHOOL CLASSES	SUCCEEDING IN COLLEGE CLASSES
The school year is 36 weeks long; some classes extend over both semesters and some don't.	The academic year is divided into two separate 15-week semesters, plus a week after each semester for exams.
Classes generally have no more than 35 students.	Classes may number 100 students or more.
You may study outside class as little as 0 to 2 hours a week, and this may be mostly last-minute test preparation.	You need to study at least 2 to 3 hours outside of class for each hour in class.
You seldom need to read anything more than once, and sometimes listening in class is enough.	You need to review class notes and text material regularly.
You are expected to read short assignments that are then discussed, and often re-taught, in class.	You are assigned substantial amounts of reading and writing which may not be directly addressed in class.
Guiding principle: You will usually be told in class what you need to learn from assigned reading.	**Guiding principle:** College is a learning environment in which you take responsibility for thinking through and applying what you have learned.

HOW IS COLLEGE DIFFERENT FROM HIGH SCHOOL?

HIGH SCHOOL TEACHERS	COLLEGE PROFESSORS
Teachers check your completed homework.	Professors may not always check completed homework, but they will assume you can perform the same tasks on tests
Teachers remind you of your incomplete work.	Professors may not remind you of incomplete work.
Teachers approach you if they believe you need assistance.	Professors are usually open and helpful, but most expect you to initiate contact if you need assistance.
Teachers are often available for conversation before, during, or after class.	Professors expect and want you to attend their scheduled office hours.
Teachers have been trained in teaching methods to assist in imparting knowledge to students	Professors have been trained as experts in their particular areas of research.
Teachers provide you with information you missed when you were absent.	Professors expect you to get from classmates any notes from classes you missed.
Teachers present material to help you understand the material in the textbook.	Professors may not follow the textbook. Instead, to amplify the text, they may give illustrations, provide background information, or discuss research about the topic you are studying. Or they may expect you to relate the classes to the textbook readings.

HOW IS COLLEGE DIFFERENT FROM HIGH SCHOOL?

HIGH SCHOOL TEACHERS	COLLEGE PROFESSORS
Teachers often write information on the board to be copied in your notes.	Professors may lecture nonstop, expecting you to identify the important points in your notes. When professors write on the board, it may be to amplify the lecture, not to summarize it. Good notes are a must.
Teachers impart knowledge and facts, sometimes drawing direct connections and leading you through the thinking process.	Professors expect you to think about and synthesize seemingly unrelated topics.
Teachers often take time to remind you of assignments and due dates.	Professors expect you to read, save, and consult the course syllabus (outline); the syllabus spells out exactly what is expected of you, when it is due, and how you will be graded.
Teachers carefully monitor class attendance.	Professors may not formally take roll, but they are still likely to know whether or not you attended.
Guiding principle: High school is a teaching environment in which you acquire facts and skills.	**Guiding principle:** College is a learning environment in which you take responsibility for thinking through and applying what you have learned.

How is college different from high school?

TESTS IN HIGH SCHOOL	TESTS IN COLLEGE
Testing is frequent and covers small amounts of material.	Testing is usually infrequent and may be cumulative, covering large amounts of material. You, not the professor, need to organize the material to prepare for the test. A particular course may have only 2 or 3 tests in a semester.
Makeup tests are often available.	Makeup tests are seldom an option; if they are, you need to request them.
Teachers frequently rearrange test dates to avoid conflict with school events.	Professors in different courses usually schedule tests without regard to the demands of other courses or outside activities.
Teachers frequently conduct review sessions, pointing out the most important concepts.	Professors rarely offer review sessions, and when they do, they expect you to be an active participant, one who comes prepared with questions.
Guiding principle: Mastery is usually seen as the ability to reproduce what you were taught in the form in which it was presented to you, or to solve the kinds of problems you were shown how to solve.	**Guiding principle:** Mastery is often seen as the ability to apply what you've learned to new situations or to solve new kinds of problems.

How is College Different from High School?

GRADES IN HIGH SCHOOL	GRADES IN COLLEGE
Grades are given for most assigned work.	Grades may not be provided for all assigned work.
Consistently good homework grades may raise your overall grade when test grades are low.	Grades on tests and major papers usually provide most of the course grade.
Extra credit projects are often available to help you raise your grade.	Grades on tests and major papers usually provide most of the course grade.
Initial test grades, especially when they are low, may not have an adverse effect on your final grade.	Watch out for your first tests. These are usually "wake-up calls" to let you know what is expected--but they also may account for a substantial part of your course grade. You may be shocked when you get your grades.
You may graduate as long as you have passed all required courses with a grade of D or higher.	You may graduate only if your average in classes meets the departmental standard--typically a 2.0 or C.
Guiding principle: Effort counts. Courses are usually structured to reward a "good-faith effort.	**Guiding principle:** Results count. Though "good-faith effort" is important in regard to the professor's willingness to help you achieve good results, it will not substitute for results in the grading process.

Used with permission from the Altshuler Learning Enhancement Center at Southern Methodist University http://smu.edu/alec/tranisition.asp

Terms for English 1101, 1102, and 1102M

Students in English 1101 and 1102/1102M should become familiar with the following terms.

Terms for English 1101

abstract language
adjectives
adverbs
affordances
agreement
antecedent
appositive
audience

claim
clause
coherence
concrete language
conjunctions
connotation
counterargument

deductive reasoning
denotation
diction
documentation
drafting

editing
emphasis
ethos
evidence

fallacy
figurative language
freewriting

generalization

inductive reasoning

jargon

logos

modifier

nouns

opinion

paragraph development
parallelism
paraphrase
pathos
phrase
plagiarism
predicate
prepositions
pronouns
punctuation

quotations

revising

specific language
subject
summary
support

thesis statement
tone
topic sentence
transition

unity

verbs

Terms for English 1102/1102M

alliteration
allegory
assonance

characters
climax
connotations

denotations
diction
dramatic monologue

end stops
enjambment
ethos

figures of speech
first person
foot

genre

iamb
imagery
Italian sonnet

magic realism
metaphor

narrative

omniscient author

persona
plot
point of view
protagonist

quatrain

realism
rhyme
rhythm

schemes
script
setting
simile
speaker
stage directions
style
symbol and symbolism
syntax

tone
trochee

unreliable narrator

voice